C000279193

Blackstone's Guide to

WORKING TIME

King's Coˡ

Inf ↑ ˢ

Blackstone's Guide to
WORKING TIME

Gwyneth Pitt

and

John Fairhurst

BLACKSTONE
PRESS LIMITED

First published in Great Britain 1998 by Blackstone Press Limited,
Aldine Place, London W12 8AA. Telephone 0181-740 2277

© Gwyneth Pitt and John Fairhurst, 1998

ISBN: 1 85431 870 5

Brtish Library Cataloguing in Publication Data
A CIP catalogue record for this book is available from the British Library

WITHDRAWN

FROM

KING'S COLLEGE LONDON
LIBRARIES

26 AUG 1999

7979

KI 8
PIT
1998

Typeset by Style Photosetting Ltd, Mayfield, East Sussex
Printed by Ashford Colour Press, Gosport, Hampshire

All rights reserved. No part of this book may be reproduced or transmitted in
any form or by any means, electronic or mechanical, including photocopying,
recording, or any information storage or retrieval system without prior permission
from the publisher.

Contents

Preface

When Margaret Thatcher signed the Single European Act in 1986, introducing qualified majority voting in the European Community, she can scarcely have realised that she was enabling the kind of intervention in the relationships of employers and workers which the Working Time Regulations represent. Such wholesale regulation of fundamental elements of the working relationship was anathema to a Conservative Government, as was indicated by their attempt first, to have the Working Time Directive quashed and secondly, to take the narrowest possible approach to implementation. The difficulties in recognising the legitimate interests of employers and workers to regulate their own affairs while ensuring compliance with the letter and spirit of the Working Time Directive and the Young Workers Directive have meant that the Labour Government too has had its problems in transposing their requirements into British law.

The Working Time Regulations have now arrived, almost two years late, and with such limited time between their drafting and their coming into force that Parliament has had almost no opportunity to review them and employers report significant problems in making the necessary rapid response. The problems are compounded by the fact that, on many crucial points, the Regulations merely copy out the terms of the Directives, although the meaning of these is far from clear.

In this book we have attempted to set out clearly the requirements of the Regulations, to relate them to practical working issues and to clarify as far as possible the difficult areas. Where certainty is impossible, we have indicated the potential arguments and analogies which may commend themselves to tribunals or courts, and strategies which may be adopted to deal with present issues.

In an era when employment law is always subject to rapid and extensive change, the Working Time Regulations represent one of the most far-reaching reforms of the content of working relationships. We hope that this guide will assist workers and employers in negotiating the maze.

Gwyneth Pitt
John Fairhurst
October 1998

Table of Cases

General Notes

The articles of the Treaty establishing the European Community ('EC Treaty') will be renumbered when the Treaty of Amsterdam ('ToA') comes into force (see art. 12 of and the annex to the ToA). Throughout this book, references to the post-ToA number are included in square brackets after the pre-ToA number.

Industrial tribunals have been renamed employment tribunals as from 1 August 1998 under the Employment Rights (Dispute Resolution) Act 1998, s. 1, and are referred to by their new name in this book.

Chapter One
Introduction

ADOPTION OF THE WORKING TIME DIRECTIVE AND YOUNG WORKERS DIRECTIVE

Although at its inception in 1958 the European Community was primarily an economic community, at a European Summit in Paris in October 1972, the Council of Ministers agreed a communiqué attaching as much importance to action in the social field as to the achievement of economic union. The Commission subsequently drafted an action plan which was approved by the Council of Ministers in January 1974 (OJ 1974 C13/74). The ensuing Social Action Programme proposed more than 30 measures over a period of three to four years. Although there was no specific proposal for a measure regulating working time within the Action Programme itself, this programme became the foundation stone for such a measure. In 1975 the Council of Ministers adopted a recommendation for a 40-hour week and four weeks' annual leave. This was followed in 1979 by a Council resolution on the adjustment of working hours, as regards, *inter alia*, overtime and total annual working hours. Although neither a recommendation nor a resolution is legally enforceable, this action clearly established the Member States' commitment to the regulation of working time.

However, with the election of a Conservative government in the UK in 1979, no further progress was made in the short term, because the legislative base for the adoption of social policy legislative measures (art. 100 [art. 94] or art. 235 [art. 308] EC Treaty) required a unanimous vote by the Council of Ministers. The Commission's proposal for a recommendation on the reduction and reorganisation of working time was blocked by the UK in 1983.

This period of inactivity terminated as a result of the Single European Act 1986. The Act amended the founding EC Treaty and came into force during 1987. Mrs Thatcher's government was very keen that the internal market be completed and thus rid the Community of all remaining obstacles to free trade. In order for the policy to be implemented by 1 January 1993, the legislative process for the adoption of measures directly affecting the internal market was amended. Article 100a [art. 95] provided for the Council of Ministers to adopt internal market measures by a qualified majority rather than unanimously under art. 100 [art. 94]. At Mrs Thatcher's insistence, art. 100a(2) [art. 95(2)] provided that measures 'relating to the rights and interests of employed persons' were excluded, in an attempt to prevent social policy being adopted by a qualified majority. However, in the horse-trading that ensued in the negotiations leading up to the adoption of the Single European Act, Mrs Thatcher agreed to the insertion of a new art. 118a [art. 137] which enabled Directives to be adopted by a qualified majority rather than unanimously, provided they related to the improvement of the health and safety of workers.

After this, the Commission issued a Health and Safety Action Programme in 1987 proposing a long list of Directives. In 1989 the Framework Health and Safety Directive 89/391/EEC (OJ 1989 L183/1) was adopted by the Council of Ministers. It provided for the adoption of a series of 'daughter' Directives covering specific risks. However, the Working Time Directive and Young Workers Directive were not among these.

Later in 1989 the European Community Charter on the Fundamental Social Rights for Workers (COM(89) 568) was signed by all of the then 12 Member States with the exception of the UK. It is a formal declaration and has no legally binding force, but it was supported by an Action Programme containing 47 proposals for legislative instruments (many of which have now been adopted). Articles 7 and 8 of the Charter concerned the improvement of living and working conditions with a specific reference to the duration and organisation of working time and the creation of rights to a weekly rest period and annual paid leave. Articles 20 to 23 were concerned with the protection of children and adolescents.

Seven months after the adoption of the Charter, the Commission proposed a Directive to regulate working time, under the health and safety provisions of art. 118a EC Treaty [art. 137] (OJ 1990 C254/4). It proposed minimum daily, weekly and yearly rest periods: a daily rest period of 11 consecutive hours in every period of 24 hours; one rest day in every seven-day period, to follow on from the 11-hour daily rest period, the average to be calculated over a reference period of not more than 14 days; and an annual paid holiday, the duration of which was to be determined in accordance with national practices.

While the Council of Ministers ultimately decide whether or not a Directive is adopted, the legislative procedure for the adoption of Directives under art. 118a [art. 137] (the cooperation procedure) requires the European Parliament to have two readings of the proposal and enables it to make amendments. Any amendments have to be accepted unless rejected by the Council on a unanimous vote.

The Economic and Social Committee delivered an opinion on the proposed Directive which was considered by the European Parliament during 1991 (OJ 1991 C60/26), following which the proposed Directive received its first reading in the Parliament. Substantial amendments were made, including: the introduction of a minimum four-week annual holiday; a work-free weekend; and a maximum average working week of 48 hours calculated over a two-week period (OJ 1991 C72/86). The Commission responded by revising its original proposal to increase the daily rest period to 12 hours and to specify a minimum annual paid holiday of four weeks. However, it failed to accept many of the other amendments, including the 48-hour maximum working week. It was over two years later before the Ministers of Social and Labour Affairs finally adopted a 'common position', the UK abstaining. This common position included all the main provisions of the final Directive. The common position returned to the Parliament for a second reading, following which the Working Time Directive was formally adopted by the Council of Ministers on 23 November 1993, with an implementation date of 23 November 1996 (Council Directive 93/104/EC (OJ 1993 L307/18)). Eleven of the then 12 Member States voted in favour; the UK abstained and indicated that it would challenge the choice of legal base.

The Young Workers Directive was proposed by the Commission in 1992 (OJ 1992 C84/7), again under the health and safety provisions of art. 118a [art. 137]. The Economic and Social Committee delivered an opinion on the proposed Directive (OJ 1992 C313/70) following which it was considered by the European Parliament for the first time (OJ 1993 C21/167).

The Council of Ministers adopted a 'common position' on 23 November 1993, during the same meeting at which it had formally adopted the Working Time Directive. Following a second reading by the Parliament in 1994 (OJ 1994 C91/89) the Young Workers Directive was formally adopted by the Council on 22 June 1994 with an implementation date of 22 June 1996 (Council Directive 94/33/EC (OJ 1994 L216/12)). However, in the case of some of the provisions relating to maximum weekly hours and night work, the UK was granted a four-year opt-out, with the possibility of a further extension.

THE UK's CHALLENGE TO THE WORKING TIME DIRECTIVE

On 8 March 1994 the UK brought an action under art. 173 EC Treaty [art. 230] for the annulment of the Directive and, in the alternative, the annulment of arts 4, 5 (sentences 1 and 2), 6 (para. 2) and 7. The second sentence of art. 5 provided that the minimum weekly rest period should 'in principle include Sunday'. The ECJ delivered its judgment on 12 November 1996 (*UK* v *Council of the European Union* (case C-84/94) [1996] ECR I-5755). In support of its action, the UK relied on four pleas:

(a)   defectiveness of the legal base of the Directive;
(b)   breach of the principle of proportionality;
(c)   misuse of powers; and
(d)   infringement of essential procedural requirements.

Defective legal base

The main thrust of the UK's argument centred around the first plea that the Directive was not concerned with the improvement of the health and safety of workers and therefore should not have been adopted under art. 118a [art. 137]. It was contended that the correct legal base was either art. 100 [art. 94] or art. 235 [art. 308], which both require unanimity within the Council of Ministers.

As discussed above, art. 100 [art. 94] empowers the Council of Ministers to adopt, by unanimous vote, Directives which directly affect the establishment or functioning of the common market. Article 100a [art. 95] derogates from art. 100 [art. 94] in that it empowers the Council of Ministers to adopt Directives which directly affect the establishment or functioning of the internal market by a *qualified majority* while specifically excluding provisions 'relating to the rights and interests of employed persons'.

The UK first argued that provisions which related to the rights and interests of employed persons and which directly affected the internal or common market would as a general rule have to be enacted under art. 100 [art. 94]. The ECJ rejected this submission. It held that art. 118a [art. 137] is a more specific legal base than art. 100 [art. 94] and art. 100a [art. 95] and this is confirmed by the actual wording of art. 100a(1) [art. 95(1)] which states that its provisions apply 'save where otherwise provided in this Treaty'. Therefore the more specific legal base of art. 118a [art. 137] was to be preferred.

Secondly, the UK argued that a strict interpretation of art. 118a [art. 137] only permitted the adoption of Directives which had a genuine and objective link to the health and safety of workers and which therefore related to physical conditions and risks at the workplace only. This did not apply to measures concerning, in particular, weekly working time (art. 6 of the Directive), paid annual leave (art. 7) and rest periods (arts 4 and 5), whose connection with the health and safety of workers was tenuous. The UK's alternative plea was for the annulment of these specific provisions. This was also rejected by the ECJ, which held that a broad scope was to be given to health and safety. This was supported by reference to the constitution of the World Health Organisation (to which all the Member States belong): health is there defined as 'a state of complete physical, mental and social well-being which does not consist only in the absence of illness or infirmity'. The UK additionally argued that the reference to the adoption of 'minimum require-ments' in art. 118a(2) [art. 137(2)] only empowered the Council of Ministers to adopt measures which were at a level acceptable to all Member States, and which constituted a minimum benchmark. This was similarly rejected by the ECJ. The reference to 'minimum requirements' enabled Member States to adopt more stringent measures than those contained in the Directive, as confirmed by art. 118a(3) [art. 137(5)].

Thirdly, it was argued by the UK that art. 118a [art. 137] did not empower the Council to adopt Directives which deal with the question of health and safety in a 'generalised, unspecific and unscientific manner'. The UK supported this argument with reference to previous Directives which had been adopted under art. 118a [art. 137], which covered specific areas of activity. The ECJ likewise rejected this argument. Past practice of the Council cannot create a precedent binding on the Community institutions with regard to the correct legal basis; in any event, the Health and Safety Framework Directive 89/391/EEC (OJ 1989 L183/1), which was adopted under art. 118a [art. 137], had a general, unspecific scope.

The ECJ concluded that 'where the principal aim of the measure in question is the protection of the health and safety of workers, art. 118a [art. 137] must be used, albeit such a measure may have ancillary effects on the establishment and functioning of the internal market'.

Having set out the legal basis for the adoption of a Directive under art. 118a [art. 137], the ECJ examined whether, in the particular circumstances of this case, the Working Time Directive had been properly adopted under this article. The ECJ noted that the approach taken by the Directive, viewing the organisation of working time essentially in terms of the favourable impact it could have on the health and safety of workers, was apparent from its preamble. While it could not be denied that the Directive might affect employment, its essential and overriding objective was one of health and safety. However, the ECJ did not accept that

Sunday could be chosen as the weekly rest day (art. 5, second sentence) because it is more closely connected to the health and safety of workers than any other day of the week. The ECJ therefore upheld this part of the UK's alternative claim and the second sentence of art. 5, which could be severed from the other provisions of the Directive, was annulled.

With regard to art. 235 [art. 308], the ECJ simply noted that that article could be used as the legal basis for a measure only where no other Treaty provision conferred on the Community institutions the necessary power to adopt it, which was not the case here.

Breach of the principle of proportionality

First, the UK argued that not all measures which may 'improve' the level of the health and safety protection of workers constitute minimum requirements. This was rejected by the ECJ which reiterated the point made above that the concept of 'minimum requirements' does not limit Community action to the lowest level of protection provided by the various Member States, but means a Member State can adopt provisions more stringent than those of the Directive.

Secondly, it was argued by the UK that the application of the principle of proportionality would require the Directive's objective of safeguarding the health and safety of workers to be attained by measures which were less restrictive and involved fewer obstacles to the competitiveness of industry and the earning capacity of individuals. The ECJ held that the Council, acting as legislature, must be allowed a wide discretion where it was making social policy choices and was required to carry out complex assessments. The ECJ would only rule the measure to be disproportionate if the exercise of the Council's discretion had been vitiated by manifest error or misuse of powers, or if it had manifestly exceeded the limits of its power. This could not be proved and was therefore rejected by the ECJ.

Thirdly, the UK argued that a measure will only be proportionate if it complies with the principle of subsidiarity and it is for the Community institutions to demonstrate that the aims of the Directive could be better achieved at Community level rather than national level. The ECJ held that it had been demonstrated that Community action was necessary to adopt minimum requirements with the objective of raising the level of the health and safety protection of workers.

Misuse of powers

Misuse of powers is defined by the ECJ as the adoption of a measure with the exclusive or main purpose of achieving an end other than that stated, or evading a procedure specifically prescribed by the Treaty. The ECJ had already held that art. 118a [art. 137] was the appropriate legal base and therefore this plea was also dismissed.

Infringement of essential procedural requirements

The UK argued that the Directive was inadequately reasoned because there was a failure to demonstrate a connection between the health and safety of workers and the provisions of the Directive. Many of the provisions were concerned with improving the living and working conditions of workers, or the internal market, rather than the health and safety of workers. This was rejected: the various recitals in the preamble to the Directive clearly reasoned the connection between the provisions and the health and safety of workers. There was no necessity to include in the preamble specific references to scientific material justifying the adoption of the various provisions.

UK PARLIAMENTARY HISTORY

The judgment of the ECJ on the UK's challenge to the Working Time Directive was delivered on 12 November 1996, 11 days before the deadline for its implementation (23 November 1996). The UK's Conservative government had not taken any steps prior to the court defeat to implement it. A consultation document was issued by the Department of Trade and Industry on 6 December 1996 requesting comments by 6 March 1997 (DTI Industrial Relations Division, *A Consultation Document on Measures to Implement Provisions of the EC Directive on the Organisation of Working Time* (URN 96/1126) (Sevenoaks: DTI Publications, 1996)). The general tenor of the document was that although it was now accepted that the Directive had to be implemented the intention was that the implementing legislation should be 'carefully tailored to the circumstances of British business so as to minimise disruption and avoid undue burdens'. Or to put it more bluntly, there should be 'no gold-plating' of the Directive's requirements. A policy of minimum compliance was advocated. The Conservative government stated that it was concerned about the 'abuse' of art. 118a [art. 137] to impose social measures on the UK which undermined the opt-out from the Social Agreement. It had already proposed that at the 1997 Amsterdam Summit art. 118a [art. 137] should be amended requiring proposed Directives to be adopted by unanimity, thus giving the UK a veto over measures brought under it, and that the Working Time Directive should be deemed to have been adopted under the Social Agreement so that its provisions would cease to apply in the UK: 'The [implementing] legislation will create rights for employees which they can claim from their employer. When the Directive no longer applies, it will be the intention of the government to repeal the [implementing] legislation and remove those entitlements and obligations so that employers and employees are once again free to determine these matters for themselves.' No further action was taken by the Conservative government prior to its general election defeat on 1 May 1997.

Implementation of the Directive then became the responsibility of the incoming Labour administration, and a new consultation document and draft regulations were issued, although this was almost 12 months after its election victory (DTI Employment Relations Directorate, *Measures to Implement Provisions of the EC Directives on the Organisation of Working Time and the Protection of Young People at Work — Public Consultation* (URN 98/645) (Sevenoaks: DTI Publications, April 1998) ('the Consultation Document')). The draft regulations were designed to implement not only the Working Time Directive, but also the provisions of the Young Workers Directive which applied to adolescent workers (i.e., above minimum school-leaving age, but below 18) and which created entitlements to certain minimum rest breaks and periods, and to a health and capacities assessment if assigned to night work.

The remaining provisions of the Young Workers Directive are implemented by three separate pieces of delegated legislation:

(a)   The Health and Safety (Young Persons) Regulations 1997 (SI 1997/135), which came into force on 3 March 1997, implemented arts 6 and 7 of the Directive, placing general obligations on the employers of young workers and prohibiting children from being employed in certain 'high-risk' activities.
(b)   The Children (Protection at Work) Regulations 1998 (SI 1998/276), which came into force on 4 August 1998, implemented the provisions of the Directive which apply to children's work generally.
(c)   The Merchant Shipping and Fishing Vessels (Health and Safety) (Employment of Children and Young Persons) Regulations 1998 (SI 1998/2411)), regulate children's work on ships at sea.

The previous government had issued a consultation document on implementation of the Young Workers Directive and 60 responses were received. The original consultation document on the Working Time Directive resulted in over 300 responses and meetings between DTI officials and around 30 organisations. The Labour government took account of the views which had been expressed when formulating its draft regulations. In direct contrast to its predecessor, the government stated in the Consultation Document that it considered the two Directives 'to be an important addition to health and safety protection for workers'. Although it favoured 'maximum flexibility in implementation' it did not believe this should be 'at the expense of fair minimum standards and the proper protection of workers from risks of excess working time leading to stress, fatigue and risks to health and safety'. The government stated that the Directives would provide protection to 'the most vulnerable employees' and was in line with its wider policy of promoting family-friendly employment:

Combining paid work and parenting, or caring for dependants, is a constant juggling act — particularly for women. Being a parent and a worker is not easy and working parents need as much support as possible. The 'long hours' culture has historically not only created barriers to work for women with caring responsibilities, but has also prevented many men from taking an active role in their children's upbringing. Providing limits on working hours, minimum rest periods from work and an entitlement to paid annual leave will help working parents to spend more time with their children and so balance their home and work commitments more successfully. (paras 8–10.)

Following the consultation exercise, the draft regulations were amended and the finalised regulations were made pursuant to the European Communities Act 1972, s. 2(2) and laid before Parliament on 30 July 1998. The Working Time Regulations 1998 (SI 1998/1833) came into force on 1 October 1998, almost two years after the Working Time Directive should have been implemented and over two years late in the case of the Young Workers Directive (except for the provisions relating to children's maximum weekly hours and night work, for which the UK had secured an extended implementation period to 22 June 1998).

SUMMARY OF THE MAIN PROVISIONS OF THE REGULATIONS

The Working Time Regulations 1998 apply to workers over the minimum school-leaving age; some special provisions apply to workers who are over the minimum school leaving age but under 18 (referred to as 'adolescent workers' in the Young Workers Directive and 'young workers' in the Regulations; their meaning is the same).

The Regulations set a weekly working hour limit of an average 48 hours. The standard averaging period is 17 weeks, but this can be extended to 26 weeks if the workers are covered by stipulated derogations or up to 12 months by agreement between the employer and workers. Individuals can voluntarily agree to work in excess of this limit.

Special provisions apply to night workers. There is a limit of an average of eight hours for each 24 hours, calculated over a 17-week period, although this period can be modified or excluded if one of the stipulated derogations applies or if an agreement is made between the employer and workers. Night workers whose work involves special hazards or heavy physical or mental strain are subject to an eight-hour limit in any 24-hour period without exception. Adult night workers are entitled to a free health assessment (a young worker to a health and capacities assessment) before being required to perform night work, and at regular intervals thereafter.

Adult workers are entitled to one day off each week (young workers to two days off), 11 consecutive hours rest per day (young workers 12 hours), and 20 minutes rest break if the working day is longer than six hours (young workers 30 minutes rest if the working day is longer than $4\frac{1}{2}$ hours). All are subject to derogations in certain circumstances.

Workers are entitled to three weeks' paid annual leave, rising to four weeks' on 23 November 1999. For new workers, this entitlement will not arise until a 13-week qualifying period has been completed.

Regulatory Guidance

The Department of Trade and Industry has issued general guidance ('Regulatory Guidance') on the Regulations which it states 'should not be regarded as a complete and authoritative statement of the law'. Presumably it will be referred to by courts and tribunals in interpreting the Regulations, although clearly they need not accept any views there stated. Reference is made to the Regulatory Guidance as appropriate in subsequent chapters.

Chapter Two
Enforcement of Community Law in the UK

The Working Time Regulations 1998 are intended to implement the EC Working Time Directive and to implement partially the EC Young Workers Directive. However, there may be circumstances where an individual may seek to enforce the terms of the Directives themselves. There are two main situations where this could arise. First, it may transpire that the Regulations have incorrectly transposed the Directives and therefore it may be necessary to rely upon the provisions of the Directives rather than the Regulations. Secondly, during the period 23 November 1996 to 30 September 1998 in the case of the Working Time Directive and 22 June 1996 to 30 September 1998 in the case of the Young Workers Directive, the Directives had not been transposed, as required by art. 189(3) [art. 249(3)] EC Treaty. For the provisions of the Young Workers Directive relating to maximum weekly hours and regulation of night work, for which the UK secured an extended time for implementation, the period of contravening non-implementation is 22 June 1998 to 30 September 1998. Therefore, during these periods, any action to indicate rights conferred by the Directives could only be pursued by invoking the provisions of the Directives themselves.

The EC Treaty does not make provision for the direct enforcement of Directives in the national courts of the Member States. However, the ECJ has developed the principles of direct effect and indirect effect, which provide for the enforcement of Community law in the courts of the Member States, and the principle of State liability, which enables damages to be recovered from a Member State which has acted in breach of Community law.

SUPREMACY OF COMMUNITY LAW

Nowhere in the EC Treaty is there a reference to the supremacy of Community law. However, the ECJ has consistently held that this principle of supremacy is implied into the Treaty (see *Costa* v *ENEL* (case 6/64) [1964] ECR 585); the principle is now firmly entrenched and accepted by national courts.

PRINCIPLE OF DIRECT EFFECT

The ECJ developed the principle of direct effect (or direct enforcement) in *Van Gend en Loos* v *Nederlandse Administratie der Belastingen* (case 26/62) [1963]

ECR 1, but limited its scope to provisions which were 'sufficiently precise and unconditional'. This has been applied quite flexibly by the ECJ and has resulted in articles of the EC Treaty and provisions of Directives being held to be directly effective in circumstances where a national court could have been excused for coming to the opposite conclusion. The following cases give an indication of the ECJ's approach.

Sufficiently precise

In *Van Duyn* v *Home Office* (case 41/74) [1974] ECR 1337 the ECJ held that art. 3(1) of the Residence and Public Policy, Security and Health Directive 64/221/EEC, which provides that 'measures taken on the grounds of *public policy* or of *public security* shall be based exclusively on the personal conduct of the individual concerned' (emphasis added) was sufficiently precise to be capable of having direct effect, despite the fact that the scope of 'public policy' and 'public security' would require determination by the ECJ.

Similarly, in *Defrenne* v *SABENA* (case 43/75) [1976] ECR 455 the ECJ held that art. 119 EC Treaty [art. 141] which set out a principle that men and women 'should receive equal pay for equal work' was sufficiently precise to be capable of having direct effect despite the fact that the scope of 'equal pay' and 'equal work' would likewise have to be determined by the ECJ.

Unconditional

A Community provision is 'unconditional' where it is not subject, in its implementation or effects, to any additional measure by either the Community institutions or Member States.

In *Van Gend en Loos* v *Nederlandse Administratie der Belastingen* (case 26/62) [1963] ECR 1 art. 12 EC Treaty [art. 25] was held to be unconditional because it imposed a negative obligation on Member States to 'refrain from introducing between themselves any new customs duties on imports and exports . . . and from increasing those which they already apply in their trade with each other'; it was not qualified by any reservation on the part of the Member States which would make its implementation conditional upon a positive legislative measure enacted under national law. This case can be contrasted with *Costa* v *ENEL* (case 6/64) [1964] ECR 585, in which it was held that art. 102 EC Treaty [art. 97] was not unconditional. Article 102 [art. 97] provides that where a Member State intends to adopt or amend its laws in a way that may cause distortion of the conditions of competition in the common market, there is an obligation of prior consultation between the Member State and the Commission. It was held that this was not unconditional because it was subject to additional measures in the form of 'prior consultation' and therefore was not capable of having direct effect.

Directives — 'sufficiently precise and unconditional'

The fact that a Directive requires Member States to perform a positive act to implement it does not in itself prevent it from being capable of being unconditional.

The ECJ held in *Francovich* v *Italy* (cases C-6 and 9/90) [1991] ECR I-5357 that in the case of employment-related Directives in general, in order to be sufficiently precise and unconditional, it is necessary to be able:

(a) to identify the persons who are entitled to the right;
(b) to ascertain the content of that right; and
(c) to identify the person or body liable to provide that right.

A similar approach was adopted by the ECJ in *Kampelmann* v *Landschaftsverband Westfalen-Lippe* (cases C-253 to 258/96) [1998] ECR I-6907, in which it was held that art. 2(2)(c) of Council Directive 91/583/EEC, which imposed an obligation on employers to inform their employees of the conditions applicable to their contract or employment relationship, was sufficiently clear and precise to be capable of having direct effect.

The *Francovich* case concerned Council Directive 80/987/EEC on protection of employees on their employers' insolvency. The persons entitled to the rights under this Directive were employees (art. 2(2) of the Directive refers to national law for the definition of the terms 'employee' and 'employer'). The ECJ held this was sufficiently precise and unconditional to allow a national judge to ascertain whether an applicant had the status of employee under national law and whether the applicant was excluded from the scope of the Directive under the specific exclusions set out therein.

The content of the right was more problematic. In implementing the Directive, the Member State was given a number of choices, which included:

(a) Choice of date from which the payment of wages would accrue; as a result Member States could limit the payment of wages to periods of three months or eight weeks.

(b) A discretion to set a liability ceiling so that payment of wages would not exceed a certain sum.

Given these legislative choices it would appear that the Directive was not unconditional or sufficiently precise. However, the ECJ held that it was possible to calculate the *minimum* guarantee provided by the Directive which would impose the least burden on the body liable to provide the benefit (i.e., the 'guarantee institution'). With regard to the discretion to set a liability ceiling, the ECJ held that this discretion would not be available unless the Member State had actually implemented the Directive and taken advantage of the derogation in its implementing legislation.

The identity of the person or body liable to provide the benefit was subject to the Member State making a legislative choice as to whether the body should be public or private, or whether it would be publicly or privately funded. Under the Directive, Member States enjoyed a wide discretion with regard to the functioning and financing of the 'guarantee institution'. The Member State had to identify the institution which would be liable to provide the benefit. The ECJ held this provision was not sufficiently precise or unconditional and therefore the Directive was not capable of having direct effect.

In *Shevlane* v *Mid-Kent College of Higher and Further Education* (6 March 1998 EAT 242/98 unreported) a lecturer was dismissed prior to the Working Time

KING'S COLLEGE LONDON LIBRARY

Directive being implemented in the UK. He claimed three weeks' holiday pay pursuant to his entitlement under art. 7 of the Directive. An industrial tribunal held that the provisions of the Directive were not sufficiently precise and unconditional to be capable of having direct effect and therefore dismissed his complaint. He appealed to the EAT which held that he had an arguable case and his appeal could proceed to a full hearing. If the EAT decides that the Directive is capable of having direct effect (i.e., it is sufficiently precise and unconditional) then, applying the principles espoused by the ECJ in the *Francovich* case, in the period during which the UK had failed to implement the Directive the option to reduce the right to paid annual leave from four weeks to three weeks could not be relied upon, because the UK had not exercised its discretion to take advantage of this option.

Limits to the direct effect of Directives

Although the ECJ has recognised that Directives may have direct effect, it has limited the scope of the principle by providing that they may only have vertical direct effect, in that they can only be enforced against the State or an emanation of the State (*Marshall* v *Southampton and South West Hampshire Area Health Authority* (case 152/84) [1986] ECR 723 and reaffirmed in *Dori* v *Recreb Srl* (case C-91/92) [1994] ECR I-3325).

In *Foster* v *British Gas plc* (case C-188/89) [1990] ECR I-3133 the ECJ developed a test to be applied to ascertain if the body against which a Directive is sought to be enforced is an 'emanation of the State':

> . . . a body, whatever its legal form, which has been made responsible, pursuant to a measure adopted by the State, for providing a public service under the control of the State and has for that purpose special powers beyond those which result from the normal rules applicable in relations between individuals *is included* in any event among the bodies against which the provisions of a Directive capable of having direct effect may be relied upon (at pp. 3348–9, emphasis added).

The three criteria can be summarised as:

(a)   provision of a public service;
(b)   under State control; and
(c)   having special powers.

Applying this test, the House of Lords held that British Gas (pre-privatisation) was an emanation of the State against which the Equal Treatment Directive 76/207/EEC could be enforced. Three important post-*Foster* cases in the UK have considered the concept of emanation of the State and the application of the *Foster* test.

In *Rolls-Royce plc* v *Doughty* [1992] ICR 538 the Court of Appeal held that Rolls-Royce could not be said to have been made responsible for providing a public service, pursuant to a measure adopted by the State; nor was there any evidence that Rolls-Royce possessed or exercised any 'special powers'. Accordingly, Doughty could not enforce the Equal Treatment Directive against Rolls-Royce, because Rolls-Royce was deemed not to be an emanation of the State, even though the government held all the shares in Rolls-Royce at the material time.

Griffin v *South West Water Services Ltd* [1995] IRLR 15 centred around the question of whether the provisions of the Collective Redundancies Directive 75/129/EEC could be enforced directly against the privatised company, South West Water ('SWW'). The High Court first considered the question of whether SWW was an emanation of the State. It was common ground between the parties that the first criterion, the 'public service' condition, and the third criterion, the 'special powers' condition, were fulfilled. The crucial question was whether or not the second criterion, the 'State control' condition, was satisfied. It was possible to point to a number of statutory powers available to the Secretary of State and the Director General of Water Services and conclude that the provision of water and sewerage services was under the control of the State, thus fulfilling the 'control' criterion. The three *Foster* criteria being satisfied, SWW was an emanation of the State and so a body against which the Directive was capable of being enforced.

The third case, *National Union of Teachers* v *Governing Body of St Mary's Church of England (Aided) Junior School* [1997] ICR 334, concerned the direct enforcement of the Acquired Rights Directive 77/187/EEC. It was common ground that, at the material time, English law would not assist the applicants. In the Court of Appeal Schiemann LJ quite correctly recognised that the ECJ had not established a test which could be applied to all situations, because in *Foster* v *British Gas plc* the ECJ had stated that a body which satisfied the three criteria 'is included among' persons against whom a Directive could be enforced; it was not intended to be an exclusive formula. Schiemann LJ said that the EAT was wrong in applying the *Foster* test as if it were a statutory definition. He was not satisfied that the governing body had 'special powers' but nevertheless held that it was an emanation of the State. He was influenced by the financial benefit accruing to the local education authority (a State body) if the appeal was dismissed. The local education authority was responsible for redundancy payments to the dismissed teachers by virtue of the Education Reform Act 1988, s. 46. The reason for the ECJ declaring that Directives are capable of being enforced against the State or its emanations is that the State should not be in a position to benefit (financially or otherwise) from its own failure to comply with its Community law obligations; art.189 EC Treaty [art. 249] requires a Member State to implement a Directive within the time period laid down within the Directive. Schiemann LJ therefore departed from a strict application of the *Foster* test, preferring to address the question on the basis that the State should not benefit from its own failure to implement a Directive.

In *Kampelmann* v *Landschaftsverband Westfalen-Lippe* (cases C-253 to 258/96) [1998] ECR I-6907 the ECJ held that in accordance with its *Foster* v *British Gas plc* judgment:

> . . . a Directive . . . may . . . be relied on against organisations or bodies which are subject to the authority or control of the State *or* have special powers beyond those which result from the normal rules applicable to relations between individuals, such as local or regional authorities *or* other bodies which, irrespective of their legal form, have been given responsibility, by the public authorities and under their supervision, for providing a public service (emphasis added).

Although the ECJ stated that this judgment was in line with its *Foster* judgment, it represents an important departure. In *Foster* the three criteria were stated to be cumulative, whereas in the *Kampelmann* judgment the ECJ sets out the criteria as alternatives. If this is subsequently reaffirmed by the ECJ as a departure from *Foster* then the bodies and organisations against which a Directive may be capable of having direct effect will be extended; arguably pre-privatised Rolls-Royce would be an emanation of the State, applying *Kampelmann*, because as 100% shareholder the government was in a position to exert authority or control over Rolls-Royce.

For a Directive, therefore, the position is that if it is sufficiently precise and unconditional it can be enforced against the State or an emanation of the State and any inconsistent national law will be overridden in accordance with the concept of Community law supremacy.

Before turning to the principle of indirect effect, some important procedural issues relating to direct effect need to be considered.

An equivalent claim

In *Comet BV* v *Produktschap voor Siergewassen* (case 45/76) [1976] ECR 2043 the ECJ was asked whether a national limitation period could operate to defeat an individual's action based upon directly effective Community rights. The ECJ held that while Community law provided the individual with enforceable rights it was for national law to provide the machinery and procedures whereby these rights could be enforced. However, in an attempt to ensure that this discretion was not open to abuse, and to introduce some uniformity into enforcement throughout the Community, the ECJ placed two limitations on this procedural freedom. First, the ECJ stated that the procedures applied must not be any less favourable than those which attach to *similar* claims in the national legal system. Secondly, the procedures must not make it impossible in practice to enforce Community rights. Accordingly, in enforcing Community rights in the UK, the national courts will apply national rules and procedures applying to an equivalent claim. These rules and procedures will include limitation periods and remedies. However, these rules and procedures can only be applied if they do not make it impossible in practice to exercise Community rights.

This was recently applied by the ECJ in *Magorrian* v *Eastern Health and Social Services Board* (case C-246/96) [1998] ECR I-7153. The case concerned female psychiatric nurses in Northern Ireland who switched from full-time to part-time working because of family commitments. For that reason they did not qualify for an enhanced pension at the age of 50, which they would have been entitled to had they remained full-time. In *Barber* v *Guardian Royal Exchange Assurance Group* (case C-262/88) [1990] ECR I-1889 the ECJ held that art. 119 EC Treaty [art. 141] required equal treatment in the matter of occupational pensions, but that pension *benefits* only had to be equalised from the date of its judgment (17 May 1990). In *Vroege* v *NCIV Instituut voor Volkshuisvesting BV* (case C-57/93) [1994] ECR I-4541 and *Fisscher* v *Voorhuis Hengelo BV* (case C-128/93) [1994] ECR I-4583 the ECJ held that this rule did not apply to a *right of access* to a pension scheme, which could be backdated to 1976 (the date of its *Defrenne* judgment). It was held in *Magorrian* v *Eastern Health and Social Services Board* that there had been a breach of art. 119 EC Treaty [art. 141]; the issue referred to the ECJ concerned time limitations on claims. The ECJ held that this case concerned a 'right of access' to a pension scheme; whether the applicants had access to a particular part of the scheme — i.e., the enhancement arrangements. The Northern Ireland domestic legislation (and its counterpart in Great Britain) limited the backdating of equal pay claims to two years. The ECJ held that this two-year limitation rendered any action by individuals relying upon Community law *impossible* in practice, and the claims could be backdated to 1976.

The issue of limitation periods has been considered by UK courts with regard to the enforcement of part-timers' rights. In *R v Secretary of State for Employment, ex parte Equal Opportunities Commission* [1995] 1 AC 1 the House of Lords declared the qualifying thresholds for unfair dismissal claims by part-time workers to be incompatible with Community law. Following this, a vast number of complaints for unfair dismissal and/or redundancy were filed by part-time workers who had been dismissed as far back as the 1970s. The Court of Appeal considered the application of this judgment, and the three-month time limitation for the filing of an unfair dismissal complaint, in *Biggs v Somerset County Council* [1996] ICR 364 where a part-time science teacher claimed unfair dismissal in respect of the termination of her contract in 1976. At the time, she did not have sufficient continuous service to claim as a part-timer (at the time, the right not to be unfairly dismissed did not apply to those in employment for less than 21 hours weekly; she had been employed for only 14 hours per week). She lodged her complaint within three months of the House of Lords' *ex parte Equal Opportunities Commission* judgment. The Court of Appeal upheld the EAT's decision that her claim was time-barred. Since the ECJ's *Defrenne* judgment in 1976 it has been possible for individuals to rely directly on art. 119 EC Treaty [art. 141] to override inconsistent national legislation. It was therefore 'reasonably practicable' for Biggs to have made her claim within the prescribed period. Her mistake as to what her rights were was a mistake of law, not of fact. This restriction did not make it 'impossible in practice' for Biggs to enforce her Community law rights. This must be questionable, but it illustrates how domestic rules and procedures can be challenged when seeking to enforce directly effective Community law rights.

However, with regard to the enforcement of Directives rather than Treaty articles, in *Emmott v Minister for Social Welfare* (case C-208/90) [1991] ECR I-4269 the ECJ held that if a Directive had not been implemented and therefore individuals were unable to ascertain the full extent of their rights, any national limitation period would not begin to run until the Directive had been correctly transposed into national law. This has been accepted and applied in the UK by the EAT in *Cannon v Barnsley Metropolitan Borough Council* [1992] ICR 698. The *Emmott* principle was recognised by the Court of Appeal in *Biggs v Somerset County Council*, but as that case concerned the direct enforcement of a Treaty article (art. 119 [art. 141]) it held that the principle did not apply. Accordingly, prior to 1 October 1998 when the Working Time Regulations 1998 came into force, any national limitation period should be suspended when directly enforcing the Directives before a UK court or tribunal.

Remedies

With regard to remedies, the rule in *Comet BV v Produkstschap voor Siergewassen* (Case 45/76) [1976] ECR 2043 has been developed a stage further by the ECJ so that the 'impossibility' limb of the rule has been refined into an 'effectiveness' principle. This principle provides that a remedy must be effective:

(a)   to protect an individual's Community law rights; and
(b)   to deter Community law from being breached.

It is the former which is most readily applied by the ECJ.

In *R* v *Secretary of State for Transport, ex parte Factortame Ltd* (case C-213/89) [1990] ECR I-2433 the ECJ applied the effectiveness principle to order the UK courts to set aside a rule which prevented an interim injunction being granted against the Crown. The House of Lords subsequently granted an injunction to prevent an Act of Parliament being enforced against the applicants.

Marshall v *Southampton and South West Hampshire Health Authority (Teaching) (No. 2)* (case C-271/91) [1993] ECR I-4367 followed the ECJ's earlier ruling (case 152/84 [1986] ECR 723) in which it was held that Marshall could rely upon the Equal Treatment Directive 76/207/EEC in her claim that her compulsory retirement at the age of 62 constituted sexual discrimination because men could continue to work until the age of 65. Under the Sex Discrimination Act 1975 the maximum compensation at the time was £6,250; the ECJ ordered the UK to set this limit aside. Full damages must be available effectively to achieve the objectives of the Directive. The effectiveness of remedies will be considered in subsequent chapters when discussing the remedies provided under the Working Time Regulations 1998.

PRINCIPLE OF INDIRECT EFFECT

In an attempt to overcome the apparent unfairness of the inability to enforce a Directive horizontally, the ECJ developed the principle of indirect effect. In *von Colson* v *Land Nordrhein-Westfalen* (case 14/83) [1984] ECR 1891, the ECJ required national courts to interpret their national law in the light of the wording and purpose of a Directive. The ECJ stated that this duty to interpret national law so as to avoid a conflict with a Directive applied in particular where the national law had been passed to implement the Directive and where the national court was given a discretion under national law to interpret it in such a manner. This considerably weakened the concept of indirect effect and was applied by the UK courts strictly to the letter of the judgment. Only where the national legislation had been enacted to transpose a Directive (and where the implementing legislation was defective) would the UK courts apply the principle.

Three decisions of the House of Lords, *Pickstone* v *Freemans plc* [1989] AC 66, *Litster* v *Forth Dry Dock and Engineering Co. Ltd* [1990] 1 AC 546 and *Duke* v *GEC Reliance Ltd* [1988] AC 618, are illustrative of this point. In the last of these, Duke was compulsorily retired at the age of 60 by GEC Reliance in accordance with company policy that women retired at 60 whereas men only retired at 65. At the material time, under English law, the Sex Discrimination Act 1975, s. 6(2)(b), made it unlawful for any employer to discriminate against a woman employed in Great Britain 'by dismissing her or subjecting her to any other detriment'. However, s. 6(4) provided that s. 6(2) did not apply to: 'provisions in relation to death or retirement'. Section 6(4) conflicted with the Equal Treatment Directive

76/207/EEC, which provided, unconditionally, that the principle of equal treatment with regard to working conditions meant that men and women would be guaranteed the same conditions without discrimination on the grounds of sex. The House of Lords refused to interpret the 1975 Act in a manner which would avoid a conflict with the Directive because it would require distorting the clear and unambiguous wording of the Act and would thus override the intention of the sovereign Parliament. The 1975 Act was enacted prior to the adoption of the Equal Treatment Directive so it quite clearly was not enacted to implement the Directive.

This case can be contrasted with *Pickstone* v *Freemans plc* and *Litster* v *Forth Dry Dock and Engineering Co. Ltd*, where the national legislation in question had been enacted by Parliament with the clear intention of implementing specific Directives (although the UK had failed to transpose them correctly). In this situation the House of Lords was willing to distort the meaning of the implementing legislation to give effect to the wording and purpose of the Directives. This is similar to an application of the mischief rule, which states that legislation should be interpreted so as to deal with the 'mischief' which it seeks to address. In these cases the objective of the legislation was to transpose an EC Directive; the words of the legislation would therefore be interpreted in such a way as to achieve this objective, thus departing from the literal rule of legislative interpretation.

However, if the national legislation preceded the Directive, the Directive would not be given effect under the guise of statutory interpretation, if that required distorting the clear statutory intent of Parliament.

This concept of indirect effect was developed a stage further by the ECJ in *Marleasing SA* v *La Comercial Internacional de Alimentación SA* (case C-106/89) [1990] ECR I-4135. The ECJ stated that 'in applying national law, whether the provisions in question were adopted *before* or after the Directive, the national court called upon to interpret it is required to do so, so far as possible, in the light of the wording and the purpose of the Directive' (at p. 4159, emphasis added). The ECJ thus extended the indirect effect principle to a duty on national courts to interpret *all* provisions of national law in accordance with Community law as far as possible, even where the provisions were adopted before the Directive in question and where the national law was not enacted specifically to implement the Directive.

Application of the principle of indirect effect in the UK, after *Marleasing*, is usefully illustrated by the approach adopted by the House of Lords in *Webb* v *EMO Air Cargo (UK) Ltd* [1993] 1 WLR 49 (HL); (case C-32/93) [1994] ECR I-3567 which again concerned the Sex Discrimination Act 1975 and the Equal Treatment Directive 76/207/EEC, which applies to the same area of activity (i.e., sex discrimination) as the 1975 Act. In the House of Lords, Lord Keith of Kinkel thought it was necessary to refer the matter to the ECJ for a preliminary ruling, to ascertain if there was a breach of the Directive. The ECJ held that Ms Webb's dismissal contravened the Directive and the case was then referred back to the House of Lords. In *Webb* v *EMO Air Cargo (UK) Ltd (No. 2)* [1995] 1 WLR 1454 the House of Lords was required to ascertain if it was possible to construe the relevant provisions of the 1975 Act so as to accord with the ruling of the ECJ. Lord Keith held that it was possible to interpret the Act in a manner consistent with the Directive, without distorting the meaning of the Act, and held that Ms Webb's dismissal constituted direct sex discrimination contrary to the 1975 Act. The Act was interpreted by the House of Lords so as to accord with the wording and purpose of the Directive, without distorting its meaning.

Duke v *GEC Reliance Ltd* is not in conflict with this decision; Parliament expressly permitted the discriminatory retirement ages complained of. To have decided otherwise would have required the court to distort the clear and unambiguous wording of the Sex Discrimination Act 1975.

Indirect effect and the Working Time and Young Workers Directives

From 1 October 1998, when the Working Time Regulations 1998 came into force, UK courts and tribunals will comply with their *Marleasing* obligation by interpreting the Regulations so as to avoid a conflict with the Directives, even if this requires distorting the wording of the Regulations. This will be particularly useful for those who are not employed by the State or an emanation of the State and who therefore cannot directly enforce against their employer those provisions of the Directives which are sufficiently precise and unconditional.

STATE LIABILITY

Francovich v *Italy* (cases C-6 and 9/90) [1991] ECR I-5357 concerned Italy's failure to implement Council Directive 80/987/EEC on protection of employees on their employer's insolvency. As discussed above, the ECJ ruled that the Directive was not directly effective, because the nature of the institution guaranteeing workers' wages should their employer become insolvent was not 'sufficiently precise and unconditional'. However, for the first time, the ECJ held that, subject to certain conditions, an individual who has suffered damage should be able to seek compensation from a Member State which has failed to implement the provisions of a Directive. The conditions which must be satisfied before a *Francovich* claim, in respect of the total non-implementation of a Directive, can succeed are:

(a)   the result required by the Directive must include the conferring of rights for the benefit of individuals;

(b)   the content of such rights can be determined by reference to the provisions of the Directive; and

(c)   a causal link exists between the breach of the Member State's obligation to implement the Directive and the damage suffered by the persons affected.

The *Francovich* principle has been extended by the ECJ in subsequent judgments. *Brasserie du Pêcheur* v *Germany* (cases C-46 and 48/93) [1996] ECR I-1029 concerned two joined cases in which directly effective Treaty articles had been breached by Germany and the UK respectively. The ECJ distinguished *Francovich* on the basis that in *Francovich* the defaulting Member State had no discretion under art. 189 EC Treaty [art. 249]: Italy was under an obligation to implement the Directive within the stipulated time period, but chose not to, which was a flagrant and obvious breach of Community law. In the two joined cases, the national legislatures had a wide discretion in the relevant fields of activity. Where there is such a discretion, the ECJ held that three conditions must be met before liability will be imposed on the State:

(a)   the rule of law infringed must be intended to confer rights on individuals;
(b)   the breach must be *sufficiently serious*; and
(c)   there must be a direct causal link between the breach of the obligation resting on the State and the damage sustained by the injured parties.

It is the second condition which is additional to those established in *Francovich*. The ECJ stated that the decisive test for finding that a breach of Community law is 'sufficiently serious' is whether the Member State 'manifestly and gravely disregarded the limits on its discretion'. The ECJ set out a number of factors which could be taken into consideration by the national court when assessing whether or not there was a 'manifest and grave disregard' by the Member State of the limit on its discretion:

56   The factors which the competent court may take into consideration include the clarity and precision of the rule breached, the measure of discretion left by that rule to the national or Community authorities, whether the infringement and the damage caused was intentional or involuntary, whether any error of law was excusable or inexcusable, the fact that the position taken by a Community institution may have contributed towards the omission, and the adoption or retention of national measures or practices contrary to Community law.

57   On any view, a breach of Community law will clearly be sufficiently serious if it has persisted despite a judgment finding the infringement in question to be established, or a preliminary ruling or settled case law of the Court on the matter from which it is clear that the conduct in question constituted an infringement (at p. I-1150).

R v HM Treasury, ex parte British Telecommunications plc (case C-392/93) [1996] ECR I-1631 concerned the UK's incorrect implementation of a Directive, which is a situation in which a Member State does not enjoy a wide discretion (art. 189(3) EC Treaty [art. 249(3)] requires a Member State to implement a Directive within the time period laid down). In its judgment the ECJ restated the three conditions in *Brasserie du Pêcheur* v *Germany* and held that it was for the national court to determine whether or not there was a 'sufficiently serious' breach. However, because the ECJ had all the necessary facts before it, it went on to advise the national court on the determination of the factual situation. The ECJ held that one of the relevant factors was the clarity and precision of the rule breached. In this case the Directive was imprecisely worded and was reasonably capable of bearing the interpretation given to it by the UK. Moreover, the UK had acted in good faith. The ECJ noted that this interpretation was shared by other Member States and 'was not manifestly contrary to the wording of the Directive or to the objective pursued by it'. Additionally there had been no case law from the ECJ to guide the UK. The Commission had not questioned the UK's implementing legislation. In those circumstances, the ECJ held that the breach could not be regarded as 'sufficiently serious', so BT's claim for compensation failed.

R v Ministry of Agriculture, Fisheries and Food, ex parte Hedley Lomas (Ireland) Ltd (case C-5/94) [1996] ECR I-2553 concerned a breach of art. 34 EC Treaty [art. 29]. In an attempt to impose a common standard for State liability throughout the Community, the ECJ held that 'those three conditions are also applicable in the circumstances of this case'; although it acknowledged that the concept of 'sufficiently serious' breach will vary, depending upon the facts of the case. With regard to this particular case, the Court stated:

> . . . where, at the time when it committed the infringement, the Member State in question was not called upon to make any legislative choices and had only considerably reduced, or even no, discretion, the mere infringement of Community law may be sufficient to establish the existence of a sufficiently serious breach (at p. I-2613).

Dillenkofer v *Germany* (cases C-178, 179 and 188 to 190/94) [1996] ECR I-4845 concerned Germany's failure to transpose Directive 90/314/EEC (a similar situation to that in *Francovich*). In *Francovich* the ECJ did not make it a condition that the breach of Community law must be 'sufficiently serious' in order for State liability to be incurred. In this case, the ECJ held that this condition was applicable to this situation, but by the very nature of the breach (i.e., a complete disregard of the Member State's obligation under art. 189(3) EC Treaty [art. 249(3)]) the breach was sufficiently serious *per se*.

State liability and the Working Time and Young Workers Directives

Liability will differ depending upon whether the claim concerns a period before the Directives were transposed, or after.

Pre-implementation   If the Directives are not given direct effect, either because the provisions are not sufficiently precise and unconditional or because they are not sought to be enforced against the State or an emanation of the State, then *Francovich* v *Italy* (cases C-6 and 9/90) [1991] ECR I-5357 and *Dillenkofer* v *Germany* (cases C-178, 179 and 188 to 190/94) [1996] ECR I-4845 provide the basis for a claim to be made against the UK, because the UK's failure to transpose the Directives constitutes a breach which is automatically 'sufficiently serious'. It is necessary to show that the Directives create rights for individuals, the extent of which are readily identifiable, and that the worker's loss is directly related to the fact that the UK had failed to implement the Directives.

In Northern Ireland a worker sued the UK government for its failure to implement the Working Time Directive and the consequential loss he had suffered through not having any annual holiday entitlement (*R* v *Attorney-General for Northern Ireland, ex parte McHugh* (unreported)). In June 1997 the government acknowledged its breach of Community law and the action never came to trial. The worker was awarded costs against the government.

Post-implementation   What is said above about liability for pre-implementation claims applies to post-implementation claims, but the issue of 'sufficiently serious' breach is more complex with regard to a Directive which has been incorrectly transposed. This situation would be similar to *R* v *HM Treasury, ex parte British Telecommunications plc* (case C-392/93) [1996] ECR I-1631 and would depend upon a number of factors as considered above. State liability will only be an issue if UK courts and tribunals refuse to give direct or indirect effect to the Directives, but even in this situation, in the intervening period between the conflict being raised and it finally being resolved, workers may suffer loss caused directly by the UK's breach and therefore may seek recompense under this principle of State liability.

Chapter Three
Scope of the Regulations

The government's objective in implementing the Working Time Directive was stated in its Consultation Document as being 'to create a flexible labour market underpinned by minimum standards' (para. 9). However, the government has also said that flexibility should not be 'at the expense of fair minimum standards' (para. 8) and that 'greater flexibility in both working patterns and contracts must be reflected in employment legislation' (*Fairness at Work* (Cm 3968, 1998)). Both strands of policy are reflected in the approach taken in the Working Time Regulations 1998 to the question of coverage. In summary, the aim is to have a broad definition of the employment relationships which come within the ambit of the Regulations, but to take maximum advantage of the variations and derogations permitted by the Directive. It remains to be seen how successfully the balance has been achieved.

DEFINITION OF 'WORKER'

There is no definition of the term 'worker' in the Working Time Directive. The terms 'employee' and 'worker' seem to be used almost interchangeably in Directives, leaving Member States to define them. Health and safety Directives tend to use the term 'worker', which is defined in the Framework Health and Safety Directive (89/391/EEC), art. 3, as 'any person employed by an employer, including trainees and apprentices but excluding domestic servants'. The Young Workers Directive is stated to apply to 'any person under 18 years of age having an employment contract or an employment relationship defined by the law in force in a Member State and/or governed by the law in force in a Member State' (art. 2(1)). The broad definition adopted in reg. 2 of the Working Time Regulations 1998 would seem to be in accordance with this. Regulation 2(1) defines 'worker' as:

> an individual who has entered into or works under (or, where the contract has ceased, worked under)—
> (a)   a contract of employment; or
> (b)   any other contract, whether express or implied and (if it is express) whether oral or in writing, whereby the individual undertakes to do or perform personally any work or services for another party to the contract whose status is

not by virtue of the contract that of a client or customer of any profession or business undertaking carried on by the individual.

This definition is the same as the definition of 'worker' in the Employment Rights Act, s. 230(3) and originated in the Wages Act 1986. The intention is clearly to bring within the ambit of the Regulations certain self-employed people, although the limits are not entirely clear. In *Fairness at Work* the government expresses an intention that the Regulations should apply to 'all those who work for another person, not just those employed under a contract of employment' (para. 3.18; see the National Minimum Wage Act 1998, s. 54(3), which also adopts this definition of the term). To date the few reported cases on the meaning of this definition have dealt with particular classes of worker such as police officers and company directors. These are discussed below.

The Regulatory Guidance states that the Regulations 'do not apply to the genuinely self-employed'. This is a strange way of expressing the position, since one could be forgiven for assuming that the law should never treat someone as an independent contractor unless they are *genuinely* self-employed. However, it is perhaps a recognition of the reality that there are a number of marginal cases where workers have been held to be self-employed when the reality is that they are freelance or casual employees (e.g., *O'Kelly* v *Trusthouse Forte plc* [1984] QB 90).

Some light may be shed on this by the cases on the similar formulations used in the Industrial Relations Act 1971 and the anti-discrimination legislation. The Sex Discrimination Act 1975, s. 82(1) , the Race Relations Act 1976, s. 78(1), and the Disability Discrimination Act 1995, s. 68(1), all apply in the employment field not only to employees and apprentices, but also to anyone with a contract 'personally to execute any work'. In *Mirror Group Newspapers Ltd* v *Gunning* [1986] ICR 145 the Court of Appeal held that this should be tested by considering what was the dominant purpose of the contract. In that case, where a newspaper distributorship had been refused to the daughter of the retiring holder, allegedly on grounds of sex, the Court held that the dominant purpose of the contract was the efficient delivery of newspapers to newsagents rather than a requirement to do work, and that in so far as work was required, it was largely irrelevant who performed it. See also *Quinnen* v *Hovells* [1984] ICR 525, where the EAT said:

The concept of a contract for the engagement of personal work or labour lying outside the scope of the master–servant relationship is a wide and flexible one, intended by Parliament, in our judgment, to be interpreted as such (at p. 531E).

The element of personal service was similarly emphasised in *Broadbent v Crisp* [1974] ICR 248, concerning the definition of 'worker' in the Industrial Relations Act 1971, which was almost identical to reg. 2. Sir Hugh Griffiths, giving the judgment of the National Industrial Relations Court, said:

The essence of the matter is whether the contract leaves the party free to delegate the performance of the work or services to some other person or whether he must perform it himself. No one test will be conclusive, but if the personality of the contracting party is found to be of importance in the formation of the contract it is a strong pointer towards the conclusion that his personal performance of contractual obligations is envisaged by the contract (at p. 255A).

Whether the worker's personal service is the 'dominant purpose' of the contract would seem to be apt for use by analogy in the context of the Working Time Regulations 1998 also. However, while the intention of the government in framing the definition of 'worker' is to be as inclusive as possible, there may be some doubt as to whether this will be achieved in practice. It is necessary to consider certain categories of worker in more detail.

Apprentices, trainees and work experience programmes

It is abundantly clear that the Working Time Directive and the Young Workers Directive apply to trainees and apprentices (see art. 3(a) of the Framework Health and Safety Directive (89/391/EEC), which applies to the Working Time Directive and art. 8(3) of the Young Workers Directive). However, in domestic law it has been held that 'Where the primary object of the contract is teaching or learning, then there is no contract of service' (Dunn LJ in *Wiltshire Police Authority* v *Wynn* [1980] ICR 649 at p. 661A).

For this reason, reg. 42 specifically provides that a person receiving relevant training otherwise than under a contract of employment is to be regarded as a worker, with the provider of the training being regarded as the employer. This formulation seems to be sufficiently wide to deal with the sort of situation which arose in *Daley* v *Allied Suppliers Ltd* [1983] ICR 90, where the EAT held that the Race Relations Act 1976 did not protect a young trainee taking part in work experience under the Youth Opportunities Programme because her attendance for work was voluntary. In these circumstances the EAT held that there was no contract in existence at all.

'Relevant training' is defined in reg. 2(1) as 'work experience provided pursuant to a training course or programme, training for employment, or both' except where the 'immediate provider' of the training or experience is an educational institution or a training company and it is part of one of its courses. Thus the Regulations would clearly *not* apply to someone undertaking a training course at a college or university, but *would* apply to young people on National Traineeships or participating in the New Deal. What is less clear is whether students going on work experience placements for a 'sandwich year' or shorter periods, or student teachers or nurses going to schools and hospitals for practical experience would be covered. A good argument could be made that this should be regarded as relevant training on the basis that the educational institution is not the 'immediate provider' of the training in this situation, and that, as this is a health and safety measure, it should be construed widely.

Casual workers

The use of casual workers, who can be called on only when needed and who are not expected to accept every offer of work, has long been prevalent in service industries with fluctuating or seasonal demands for workers, such as hotels and catering and some agricultural work. Increasingly, however, all sorts of businesses are evincing a reluctance to employ permanent workers if their time is not likely to be fully occupied, and there has been a general expansion in the use of casual workers, who may be called on as and when they are required and who need only be paid when they actually work. The lack of reciprocal obligations, on the employer to offer work and on the worker to accept work when offered, is the hallmark of a casual work arrangement.

A more recent variant, the so-called 'zero hours contract', differs from the usual casual work arrangement in that it usually purports to place an obligation on the worker to accept work when offered, although the employer has a discretion whether to offer the work or not. In its White Paper, *Fairness at Work*, the government estimated that as many as 200,000 people work under zero hours contracts (Cm 3968, para. 3.14). Recognising the potential for abuse of such arrangements, an issue which it raised for consultation, the government nevertheless added:

> The government wishes to retain the flexibility these contracts offer business and believes that the National Minimum Wage and the Working Time Directive provide important basic protections against some of the potential abuses (para. 3.15).

It is true that the Regulations could be of particular importance for such workers in ensuring their entitlement to proper rest breaks and in curbing excessive working hours: however, this can only occur if the Regulations in fact apply to them, which is not at all clear.

The employment status of casual workers is frequently in doubt, mainly because of the lack of mutual obligations between them and their employers. Two questions arise: first, whether any individual engagement is a contract of employment, and secondly, whether the overall continuing relationship in the context of which the work takes place constitutes a 'global' or 'umbrella' contract which is itself a contract of employment.

In relation to the Working Time Regulations 1998, it may seem at first sight that there is no particular problem because the definition of 'worker' clearly covers contracts for services where the worker has an obligation to render personal service. But the difficulty arises because there is a prior question: whether or not there is a contract at all between the parties. Recently in *Cheng Yuen* v *Royal Hong Kong Golf Club* [1998] ICR 131 the Privy Council held that caddies who worked casually were merely licensees allowed to ply their trade on the club's premises, even though they were provided with uniforms by the club, received their pay from the club and were subject to its control and disciplinary procedures when they were working.

Thus one danger is that casual workers may be deemed not to have contracts at all. Even if the existence of a contract is established, the absence of mutual obligation might mean that it is regarded as merely a contract for each occasion on which the worker actually works rather than taking place in the context of a global or umbrella contract (see *Hellyer Brothers Ltd* v *McLeod* [1987] ICR 526, *Clark* v *Oxfordshire Health Authority* [1998] IRLR 125). This would mean again that many of the protections provided by the Working Time Regulations 1998, such as the right to paid annual leave, would be illusory for such workers. For example, in *Clark* v *Oxfordshire Health Authority* the applicant was a 'bank nurse', meaning that she was one of a pool of qualified nurses who could be called upon whenever there was a need. However, there was no guarantee of work and she had no legal obligation to accept work when it was offered. There was evidence that she worked with considerable regularity over a three-year period, but because of the lack of reciprocal obligations to offer and accept work the Court of Appeal held that this was a series of separate engagements rather than an overall, continuing contract. One of the factors inclining them to that view was the fact that she did not accept engagements when she wanted a holiday! It seems that the Working Time Regulations 1998 will not provide 'basic protections against some of the potential abuses' in this kind of situation.

Paradoxically, it may be that a worker has more chance of establishing a continuous contract with a zero hours contract. *Carmichael v National Power plc* [1998] IRLR 301 concerned two women employed as guides taking visitors on tours of the Blythe power station. Their contracts stated that they were employed 'on a casual as required basis'. The Court of Appeal construed this to mean that there were mutual obligations on both parties to the contract: on the part of the employer, to offer them a reasonable share of whatever guide work they had available, and on the part of the employees, to accept a reasonable amount of the work that they were offered (see also *Nethermere (St Neots) Ltd v Gardiner* [1984] ICR 612). In such circumstances, there would be a continuing contract to which the limits and entitlements provided for in the Working Time Regulations 1998 could attach.

Agency workers

Similar problems to those affecting casual workers have also been faced by agency workers seeking to rely on statutory employment protection rights. Although they will usually have an obligation to render personal service when they take on a contract offered through their agency, it is not clear that this is done in the context of a global or umbrella contract, and even if it were, who the employer would be.

For this reason, provision is made in reg. 36 to bring agency workers within the scope of the Regulations. Regulation 36 applies to any situation where an individual (the agency worker) is supplied by one party (the agent) to do work for another party (the principal), whether pursuant to a contract or some other arrangement, but the individual does not have a contract as a worker with either the agency or the principal. Provided that this is not a situation where the agency worker can be said to be providing professional services to a client or customer, reg. 36 states that the Working Time Regulations 1998 will have effect as if there were a worker's contract between the agency worker (the individual) and *either* the agent *or* the principal, according to which of them is responsible for paying the worker. (The National Minimum Wage Act 1998, s. 36, is in almost identical terms.)

Several points arise from this. First, reg. 36 must be regarded as an important extension of the scope of the Working Time Regulations 1998. In the past, agency workers have generally failed in attempts to establish their status as employees of either the agency or the client for whom they actually worked (*Wickens v Champion Employment* [1984] ICR 365; *Ironmonger v Movefield Ltd* [1988] IRLR 461; *Pertemps v Nixon* (1993 EAT/496/91 unreported)). Recently the Court of Appeal held in *McMeechan v Secretary of State for Employment* [1997] ICR 549 that an agency worker could be regarded as an employee of the agency in respect of his last specific engagement with a client, but stressed that each case would depend on its own facts. In the absence of reg. 36, then, a significant minority of workers would have been denied the protection of the Regulations.

Having said that, however, it should be noted that the ambit of reg. 36 is unclear in a number of respects. It appears that it will not apply if there *is* a worker's contract between the agency worker and either the agency or the principal. The question is whether the reference to a 'worker's contract' will be taken to be satisfied by a contract for a single engagement (as in *McMeechan* v *Secretary of State for Employment*) or whether it will be satisfied only where there is a global or overall arrangement which amounts to such a contract. Where reg. 36 does apply, the emphasis on who pays the worker as the sole criterion for deciding whether the agency or the client is to be treated as the employer for all the purposes of the Regulations may seem surprising. On the other hand, as long as agencies and their clients are aware of the position, the provision gives them ample scope to negotiate an arrangement which is satisfactory to them without risk of later upset by a court or tribunal.

Other special categories

Police In *Commissioner of Police of the Metropolis* v *Lowrey-Nesbitt* (1998) *The Times*, 29 July 1998 the EAT held that a police officer in the Metropolitan Police was an office-holder and not in an employment relationship with anyone. She was therefore not entitled to claim that there had been an unlawful deduction from her wages contrary to Part II of the Employment Rights Act because she was not a worker within the meaning of s. 230(3). To counter this, reg. 41 of the Working Time Regulations 1998 provides that holding the office of constable or appointment as a police cadet is to be treated as employment under a worker's contract, with the chief officer of police or chief constable being treated as the employer.

However, under reg. 18(c), there is an exclusion for any characteristics of police service which inevitably conflict with the provisions of the Regulations. This is considered further below.

Armed forces and Crown employment Regulation 37 extends the scope of the Regulations to all those in Crown employment, with the proviso that the Crown may not be made criminally liable for any offence under the Regulations. Where an act or omission by the Crown amounts to such an offence, the relevant court may only make a declaration that it is unlawful.

The armed forces are defined in reg. 2 as, 'any of the naval, military and air forces of the Crown'. Certain exclusions apply as for the police, and these are discussed below. Furthermore, members of the armed forces cannot present a complaint to an employment tribunal unless they have gone through internal procedures first (reg. 38), although in these circumstances they have six months in which to apply instead of the usual three (reg. 30(2)). Regulations 39 and 40 state that staff of the House of Lords and the House of Commons are covered by the Regulations.

Agricultural workers Agricultural workers are the last group still to be covered by specific minimum wage legislation. The Agricultural Wages Board survived the final abolition of wages councils by the Trade Union Reform and Employment Rights Act 1993 and retains the power to fix minimum terms and conditions for agricultural workers, including, among other things, holidays. Regulation 43 of and sch. 2 to the Working Time Regulations 1998 therefore provide that the leave year for these workers will run from 6 April each year, or the date specified in the applicable agricultural wages order, instead of 1 October, the fallback date in reg. 13, and that the dates on which leave is taken will be governed by the applicable agricultural wages order rather than by reg. 15. However, it will be possible to have different arrangements if a relevant agreement is in force, and to this extent the power of the Agricultural Wages Board is reduced.

Young workers   A 'young worker' is defined in reg. 2 as a worker aged between 15 and 18 who is over compulsory school-leaving age. (The equivalent term used in the Young Workers Directive is 'adolescent worker', with 'young person' there meaning anyone aged under 18: art. 3.) The relevance of this classification is that extra protections are applicable to young workers under the Regulations.

EXCLUDED ACTIVITIES

Article 1(3) of the Working Time Directive permitted the exclusion of certain sectors of activity, representing no doubt a compromise reflecting the particular sensitivities of different Member States. The exclusion of junior hospital doctors, for example, was the UK's special contribution to this part of the Directive. The preamble to the Directive justifies the exclusion on the basis that:

> given the specific nature of the work concerned, it may be necessary to adopt separate measures with regard to the organisation of working time in certain sectors or activities which are excluded from the scope of this Directive.

This in effect reserved the right to revisit the exclusions in the future, and in July 1997 the EC Commission published a White Paper on sectors and activities excluded from the Working Time Directive (COM (97) 334, 10046/97) considering what action should be taken to safeguard the health and safety of workers in these areas and to re-examine whether the excluded categories were wider than they needed to be. At the end of March 1998 the Commission moved to the second stage of consultation in accordance with the procedure laid down in art. 3(3) of the Agreement on Social Policy annexed to the Treaty of European Union [art. 138] and proposed that the European social partners should begin negotiations on this issue. The Commission was also required to seek the opinion of the Economic and Social Committee, which in March expressed its view that the Working Time Directive should be extended to all sectors as soon as possible. The social partners reported at the end of September 1998. Agreement was reached by the social partners in the railway and maritime sectors, but not in road transport. This means that the agreements in the rail and maritime industries will be converted into proposals to the EC Council for legislation, but in relation to road transport the buck now passes to the EC Commission to formulate proposals. Thus, while at present there are no firm legislative proposals to extend the scope of the Working Time Directive, this is likely to change in the near future.

The excluded sectors are identified in reg. 18. People working in these sectors are completely outside the protections of the Working Time Regulations, except for the provisions which relate specifically to young workers (i.e., health assessment for night work: reg. 7(2); daily rest: reg. 10(2); weekly rest: reg. 11(3), and rest breaks: reg. 12(4)).

Transport

Regulation 18(a)(i) excludes 'air, rail, road, sea, inland waterway and lake transport'. The scope of this exclusion has been one of the most hotly debated issues in relation to both the Directive and the Regulations. Contrary to the hopes of many, the Regulations here simply copy out the equivalent provision in the Directive (art. 1(3)) without further clarification.

The Conservative government's Consultation Document of December 1996 (URN 96/1126) famously opined that workers whose work had a clear connection with the transport sector would be excluded, giving as an example 'retail staff who work in an airport' (para. 3.3). This always seemed dubious, and the present government's Consultation Document specifically states that there is *no* implication that the mere location of work activity in a transport facility makes those workers subject to the exclusion (URN 98/645, para. 42). This is repeated in the Regulatory Guidance (para. 1.2.3). This interpretation is buttressed by the reference in reg. 21, derived from art. 17(2)(1)(c) of the Working Time Directive, to 'work at docks or airports' in relation to a different exclusion. The implication must be that at least some workers at docks and airports are not affected by the transport exclusion, since this provision would otherwise be otiose. The staff of W.H. Smith's Heathrow branches can breathe a sigh of relief.

It might be thought that the rationale for the exclusion of the transport sector would be the difficulty in applying working time limits and rest-break entitlements to workers who are involved in travelling (although this would not be a reason for exclusion from paid annual leave entitlements). If so, then the exclusion should be limited to workers so engaged. However, in its White Paper (COM (97) 334, 10046/97) the EC Commission expressed the view that all workers in the transport sector, even 'non-mobile' workers, were excluded. On this basis, the secretarial staff at a transport firm's headquarters would be excluded even though secretarial staff for a solicitor's firm in the same building would not be. Indeed, the Commission's invitation to the European social partners to consider this exclusion suggests that a differentiated approach, distinguishing mobile and non-mobile workers and bringing the former within the scope of the Working Time Directive, while making sector-specific arrangements for mobile workers, could be the appropriate route for reform.

The Regulatory Guidance suggests that 'workers involved in the movement of goods or people to or from a mode of transport (for example, in docks or loading/unloading on to/from road vehicles)' will not necessarily be excluded (para. 1.2.3). This is likely to depend on the identity of the employer, however. If warehouse staff employed by a furniture store have to unload lorries delivering furniture and then use fork-lift trucks to move things around in the warehouse, it seems reasonable not to regard them as employed in the transport sector. On the other hand, baggage handlers at an airport, as the Regulatory Guidance points out, are more likely to be regarded as within the transport sector if their employer is the airport, although this cannot be regarded as definite in the absence of authoritative decision. It may be that the drive to outsource services which has been such a feature of recent years may operate to some workers' advantage, since it becomes less likely that they will be employed directly by a transport sector employer and more probable that they will be able to argue that their work is merely located in a transport facility.

The Regulatory Guidance accepts that 'there are sound reasons for maintaining that some "own account" transport operations (for example, a retail chain operating a fleet of vehicles to deliver goods to its own stores)' are to be regarded as falling within the transport sector, since they are almost identical to firms solely carrying out road haulage operations in this respect (para. 1.2.3). If this were not the case, it would be comparatively easy for such companies to restructure so as to place their transport operations in a separate company, which would clearly be a transport sector employer (subject, of course, to the Transfer of Undertakings (Protection of Employment) Regulations 1981).

No doubt the precise ambit of this exclusion will give rise to some difficult cases. What about a worker who spends part of his or her time driving around on deliveries and part on non-transport activities? Or an accounts clerk for a retail chain whose time is wholly devoted to dealing with the hours and pay of its HGV drivers? It is impossible to say unless and until such cases come before courts and tribunals. A prudent employer would be advised to observe the requirements of the Regulations in respect of any workers whose position is doubtful, making use of the facility to enter relevant agreements where appropriate.

Work at sea

Sea fishing and other work at sea are excluded from the Regulations by reg. 18(a)(ii) and (iii). The reference to 'other work at sea' includes, in particular, work in the offshore oil and gas industry.

Young workers employed on ships, whose employment is governed by the Merchant Shipping Act 1995, are excluded from the Working Time Regulations by virtue of reg. 26. The relevant provisions of the Working Time Directive and the Young Workers Directive in relation to them are dealt with in the Merchant Shipping and Fishing Vessels (Health and Safety) (Employment of Children and Young Persons) Regulations 1998.

Doctors in training

Regulation 18(b) excludes the activities of doctors in training. As noted above, this group was excluded at the behest of the UK, since British hospitals are heavily dependent on junior doctors working extraordinarily long hours. This exclusion does not, of course, absolve employers from their general duty to take reasonable care for the health and safety of their employees. In *Johnstone v Bloomsbury Health Authority* [1992] QB 333 the Court of Appeal held that an express term of a junior hospital doctor's contract which provided for a basic 40-hour week and unlimited overtime (not to average more than an extra 48 hours per week!) was to be read subject to this duty. If excessive hours are damaging to the worker's health, the employer may be liable for negligence.

The Regulatory Guidance identifies the relevant grades of doctors in training as: pre-registration house officer, house officer, senior house officer, registrar, senior registrar and specialist registrar (para. 1.2.3).

Police, armed forces and civil protection services

Under reg. 18(c) the Regulations do not apply:

> where characteristics peculiar to certain specified services such as the armed forces or the police, or to certain specific activities in the civil protection services inevitably conflict with the provisions of these Regulations.

This exclusion is derived from art. 2(2) of the Framework Health and Safety Directive (89/391/EEC), incorporated by art. 1(3) of the Working Time Directive. As with the transport exclusion, the approach of the drafter of the Regulations is to copy out almost exactly the wording of art. 2(2). This is particularly unhappy here, since the wording of the article would seem to suggest that the Member State's implementing legislation should actually specify which services have characteristics conflicting with the Regulations. Unfortunately, reg. 18 is worded as if the police and armed forces are only examples of these services and that there could be others.

The exclusion applies to any characteristics of the specified services which inevitably conflict with the Regulations, but only to specific *activities* in the civil protection services which conflict. Confusingly, the civil protection services are defined in reg. 2(1) as including 'the police, fire brigades and ambulance services, the security and intelligence services, customs and immigration officers, the prison service, the coastguard, and lifeboat crew and other voluntary rescue services'. Thus the police are included in both limbs.

However, the exclusion operates only in so far as there is an inevitable conflict between the Regulations and the operational demands of the services. The Regulatory Guidance suggests that the civil protection services themselves have the responsibility for identifying the specific activities which conflict with the Regulations, but it is submitted that any such decision would be open to review in a court or tribunal.

Domestic service

There is no mention of domestic servants in the Working Time Directive, although they are expressly excluded from the scope of the Framework Health and Safety Directive (89/381/EEC, art. 3). In general, domestic servants are not covered by British health and safety legislation (Health and Safety at Work etc. Act 1974, s. 51).

Following this pattern, reg. 19 excludes domestic servants in private households from the limits on working time, including night work, health and safety assessments and pattern of work requirements. However, they are entitled to rest breaks and annual leave in accordance with the Regulations.

Unmeasured working time

Regulation 20 excludes the limits on working time and entitlements to rest breaks in respect of any worker:

> where, on account of the specific characteristics of the activity in which he is engaged, the duration of his working time is not measured or predetermined or can be determined by the worker himself.

Once again, this reproduces in almost exactly the same words, the relevant provisions of the Directive (art. 17(1)) with no attempt at clarification. The obscurity of this provision is hardly rendered less ambiguous by the addition, àgain in the same words as the Directive, of certain exemplars of this category:

> (a)   managing executives or other persons with autonomous decision-taking powers;
> (b)   family workers; or
> (c)   workers officiating at religious ceremonies in churches and religious communities.

Taken at its widest, this exception could embrace large numbers of professional workers for whom it is almost a defining characteristic that their work is delineated by the task to be performed rather than the time taken to do it. Many, if not most, will also enjoy some degree of autonomy over when, how and even where they work. Yet the vast majority of these professional workers will also be employees to whom it must be intended that the Regulations will apply. Something narrower than this therefore must be meant. The Regulatory Guidance suggests that 'this applies to workers who have complete control over the hours they work and whose time is not monitored or determined by their employer. . . . An indicator may be if the worker has discretion over whether to work or not on a given day without needing to consult their employer' (para.2.2.2). This approach, if adopted by courts and tribunals, would narrow the ambit of the exception considerably. There can be few workers whose time is not at least monitored by their employer. Contractual provisions defining the worker's obligations to work will be an important source of information on this question.

Many company directors are employees, even when they are also controlling shareholders of the company, a situation recognised as legitimate at least since *Lee v Lee's Air Farming Ltd* [1961] AC 12. In *Secretary of State for Trade and Industry v Bottrill* [1998] ICR 564 the EAT ruled that there is no rule of law preventing a director who is also a controlling shareholder from having the status of employee under s. 230 of the Employment Rights Act 1996 and thus qualifying for statutory rights such as (in this case) redundancy payments. In reaching this decision, the EAT declined to follow its earlier decision in *Buchan v Secretary of State for Employment* [1997] IRLR 80, where it was held that such a director could not qualify for statutory employment protection rights because the circumstances giving rise to a claim were under his own control as owner of the company which was his employer. In such a situation, however, it is likely that an employed director who is also the controlling shareholder would fall within the exception in reg. 20(a).

The reference to family workers presumably applies to people working in a business owned or controlled by a member of their family. It should be noted that falling into this category, as with the autonomous executive, does not of itself result in exclusion: the issue is whether the work exhibits the relevant characteristics.

In relation to workers officiating at religious ceremonies, it is worth noting that in the UK such workers are frequently not considered to work under a contract in any case, and so would fall outside the definition of worker in reg. 2 (see, e.g., *Diocese of Southwark* v *Coker* [1998] ICR 140; Brodin, (1996) 25 ILJ 211).

Workers to whom reg. 20 applies enjoy annual leave entitlements under reg. 13 and the protection of reg. 8 concerning the pattern of work.

Other special cases

Regulation 21 lists other groups of workers who are excluded from the limit on night work and entitlements to rest breaks because of the particular exigencies of their work. However, under reg. 24 they are entitled either to equivalent rest breaks or other appropriate protection measures to compensate them for the exclusion of the rest entitlements. There is also a difference in the way that the working time limit in reg. 4 applies to these groups: the reference period for measuring their average working time is extended from 17 weeks to 26 weeks (reg. 4(5)). The list of these groups is copied virtually without change from art. 17(2)(1) and (2). There are five.

Distant place of work   Where the worker's place of work and home are distant from each other or a number of places of work are distant from each other, these exclusions apply. The Regulatory Guidance suggests that this is to allow for such workers to work in longer, concentrated periods to minimise commuting, or where continual changes in the place of work make it impractical to set a pattern.

The ambit of this exception is far from clear, and an employer who wishes to rely on it should probably seek the worker's agreement to being classified in this way.

Security work   The exclusion applies to security or surveillance work requiring a permanent presence to protect property or persons.

Continuous production   Similarly, in industries where continuous service or production is required, the flexibility provided by this exception will apply. Regulation 21, following the Directive, gives a list of examples, such as hospitals, prisons, airports, utilities and broadcasting. However, it is important to note that working in such an industry does not of itself mean that the exclusion applies: it depends on whether the need for continuity is established in relation to the worker's activities.

Seasonal surge   The exception also applies to workers in industries subject to a 'foreseeable surge of activity'. Possible examples suggested in the Regulations are agriculture, tourism and postal services.

Emergencies Finally, the exception applies in case of emergencies such as exceptional events, accidents or occurrences due to unusual and unforeseeable circumstances.

CONCLUSION

The discussion of who is covered by the Working Time Regulations 1998 illustrates in microcosm many of the problems to be encountered with the Regulations in general. Too many of the key concepts are unclear, because they simply copy out the words of the Directive, without further explanation. While the Government may feel that this makes its implementation proof against attack by infraction proceedings, it is less than helpful to the millions of workers and employers affected by these rules.

Chapter Four
Limits on Working Time

INTRODUCTION

Unlike other European countries, there is no tradition of general limitations on working time in the UK. The Factories Acts in the nineteenth century fixed certain limits on the working time of women and young persons, but they did not apply to men nor to employment outside their scope. Despite having considerable influence in the framing of ILO Convention No.1 on Hours of Work in 1919, which provided for an eight-hour day and a 48-hour week, the UK declined to sign it.

This can be explained in terms of the traditional British preference for voluntary collective bargaining to regulate the content of the employment relationship. When industry-level bargaining was strong and supported by legal measures for extension, such as the Fair Wages Resolution, this may have been sufficient protection. However, in recent years the proportion of the workforce covered by collective bargaining arrangements has declined significantly, and where it continues to exist, such bargaining has become fragmented and is more likely to be at plant level only, making it more difficult to maintain general minimum standards.

Whatever the cause, the result is that workers in British industry have longer working hours than their counterparts in other European countries, which have long had statutory limits on working hours. In 1995 over 3.5 million employees, some 16% of the total workforce, regularly worked more than 48 hours per week. This was particularly likely to be the case in the service sector, notably hotels and distribution, banking and finance, transport and communications. In manufacturing industry, long working hours are a feature of traditional heavy industries such as engineering, metal and mining, as well as construction. As will be seen, individual workers may opt out of the limits on working time stipulated in the Working Time Regulations, so it does not follow that there will necessarily be much change in working practices. The critical question is whether workers can earn an adequate living wage with fewer hours. If not, they will continue to opt for opportunities to work extensive overtime. The level at which the national minimum wage is set is therefore likely to be crucial to the success or otherwise of the Working Time Regulations 1998 in bringing down average working hours in the UK.

WORKING TIME

Any limits on working time first of all require a definition of what counts as working time. Article 2(2) of the Working Time Directive defines 'working time' as 'any period during which the worker is working, at the employer's disposal and carrying out his activity or duties, in accordance with national laws and/or practice'. Any other time is designated a 'rest period' by art. 2(2).

The Directive definition is adopted, but also extended, in the definition in the Working Time Regulations 1998, reg. 2:

> 'working time', in relation to a worker, means—
>   (a)   any period during which he is working, at his employer's disposal and carrying out his activity or duties,
>   (b)   any period during which he is receiving relevant training, and
>   (c)   any additional period which is to be treated as working time for the purpose of these Regulations under a relevant agreement;
> and 'work' shall be construed accordingly.

Given the ambiguities in sub-para. (a) in particular, this definition is bound to give rise to difficult cases. The government's general answer to this is that sub-para. (c) enables employers and workers to reach their own agreements on what is and is not to count as working time. However, this is not a complete solution. First of all, sub-para. (c) provides only for *additional* periods of time to count as working time. In other words, it is not possible for a 'relevant agreement' (the meaning of which is discussed in the next section) to exclude from the ambit of working time anything which would otherwise fall under the definition by virtue of sub-paras (a) and (b). Hence the ambit of those sub-paragraphs standing alone must be ascertained. Secondly, there are bound to be situations where no relevant agreement has been reached.

In relation to sub-para. (a), the critical question is whether the three conditions are to be read conjunctively or not. If all three must be satisfied the concept of working time will obviously be much narrower than if only one sufficed. The presence of the word 'and' between 'at his employer's disposal' and 'carrying out his activities' does not necessarily prove that the conditions are cumulative. However, it was assumed to be so by the government in its Consultation Document (URN 98/645, para. 26) and this is also categorically stated in the Regulatory Guidance (para. 2.1.2: 'For time to be "working time" all three elements must be satisfied'). This does not preclude the possibility of courts or tribunals taking a different view. There are four particular situations where the question is likely to be acute: time spent on call, lunch and other breaks, time off in accordance with statutory rights, and travelling time. One important point made in the Consultation Document is that there is no necessary connection between paid time and working time under this definition.

On-call time

Workers may be 'on call' in a number of different situations. Nurses, firefighters and doctors may be able to spend their on-call time at home or wherever else they wish, provided that they are contactable and available to work if required. Other workers may be required to be on standby at the employer's premises, although permitted to rest or engage in recreational activities unless actually needed to work. All these workers are 'at the employer's disposal', but probably do not fulfil the other two conditions; although, as the Consultation Document pointed out, it may be difficult to say definitively what constitutes 'work':

> Many service sector jobs require workers to be at their place of work waiting until required to serve a customer (e.g. a shop assistant or a waiter): this is often an inevitable aspect of their job and they are likely to consider themselves to be working during such time (para. 26).

The Regulatory Guidance argues that time spent by on-call workers who are free to pursue their own activities is not working time; nor is time spent on call at the place of work but resting. If all three conditions in (a) have to be fulfilled, this is probably right. But it could be argued that the definition should be read as meaning *either* working *or* at the employer's disposal *and/or* carrying out his activity or duties. The worker on call who has to be at the place of work could be said to be carrying out his or her duties by being available on the premises to work, even if not actually working. It is worth noting that in some other Member States, such as Germany, the presence or otherwise of the on-call worker at the workplace is treated as the decisive criterion.

It should also be remembered that some on-call workers may not fall within the scope of the Regulations in any case (see *Clark* v *Oxfordshire Health Authority* [1998] IRLR 125, discussed in chapter 3).

Lunch and other breaks

During break times, whether paid or unpaid, the worker is not working, is not (usually) at the employer's disposal, nor carrying out his or her activity or duties. Thus it would seem unlikely that breaks will count as working time. This is the line taken by the Regulatory Guidance, which further observes that a working lunch which the worker is obliged to attend would be working time. This is more categorical than the Consultation Document, in which it was thought that there might be doubt about whether a lunch break which was part of the worker's contractual hours would be counted as working time. This raises another significant point: the definition of working time makes no specific reference to the contract in identifying working time, although the terms of the contract would obviously be relevant to each of the three conditions.

Rights to time off work

Employees have a number of rights to paid and unpaid time off work:

(a) time off for public duties (Employment Rights Act 1996, s. 51);
(b) time off to look for work (s. 52);
(c) time off for ante-natal care (s. 55);
(d) time off for employee trustees of pension schemes (s. 58);
(e) time off for employee representatives to consult on redundancy or the transfer of an undertaking (s. 61);

(f) time off for trade union duties and activities (Trade Union and Labour Relations (Consolidation) Act 1992 ss. 168–70);

(g) time off for employee safety representatives (Safety Representatives and Safety Committees Regulations 1977 (SI 1977/500); Health and Safety (Consultation with Employees) Regulations 1996 (SI 1996/1513)).

Is this time to be treated as working time? Should the same rules apply for all these rights to time off? This issue is not addressed in the Regulatory Guidance or in the government's 1998 Consultation Document. The Consultation Document produced under the Conservative government (which was, of course, committed to minimum possible compliance) expressed the view that time spent performing duties and functions in pursuance of statutory time off rights would not usually count as 'working time' (URN 96/1126, para.3.13).

If the three requirements in sub-para. (a) of the definition of 'working time' in reg. 2(1) of the Working Time Regulations 1998 are cumulative, this might appear to be correct. On the other hand, it would be strange if health and safety representatives could be expected to work from 9.00 a.m. to 2.00 p.m., then attend a safety committee from 2.00p.m. to 4.00 p.m. and then to work again from 4.00 p.m. to 5.00 p.m. without having an entitlement to any break at all. Yet if the 'time off' period is not treated as 'working time', they would not be entitled to a rest break under reg. 12 because the daily working time would not have exceeded six hours. Indeed, if this period is not treated as 'working time', the safety representatives might have a legitimate complaint that they had not been permitted to take time off work, because the safety committee meeting occurred during a 'rest period'.

The problem arises because the definition of working time in the Regulations is different from the definition of 'working hours' in the Employment Rights Act 1996, the Trade Union and Labour Relations (Consolidation) Act 1992 and the statutory instruments dealing with time off rights for safety representatives. These all define 'working hours' as 'any time when, in accordance with his contract . . . he is required to be at work' (e.g., Employment Rights Act 1996, s. 50(11), Trade Union and Labour Relations (Consolidation) Act 1992, ss. 146, 152, 246). The Working Time Regulations 1998 do not address the question of how these provisions are to be fitted together. It is submitted that in order to give effect to the purpose of both sets of provisions, time off in accordance with statutory rights must be treated as 'working time' for the purposes of the Regulations. Nor should this depend on whether or not the time off is for what could be described as a work-related activity (such as trade union duties, pension fund trustees, safety representatives or representatives for redundancy and TUPE consultation) or something which is more in the worker's personal interest (time off to look for work, ante-natal care and public duties). While it is true that the employer may have little control over the time spent on the 'personal' activities, the 'time off' element is referable to the contract of employment and so can be measured and controlled by the employer.

Travelling time

Whether or not a worker is to be regarded as 'in the course of employment' while travelling is a question which has greatly exercised the courts in relation to the vicarious liability of an employer for the negligence of employees. It is possible that there could be comparable problems over whether travel in connection with work is to be regarded as part of a worker's 'working time'.

The Regulatory Guidance expresses the view, which must be non-controversial, that time spent travelling to and from the place of work is unlikely to be working time, as the worker would neither be working nor carrying out his or her activity or duties. If a worker's job involves transport, then he or she may already be excluded from the Regulations by virtue of the transport sector exemption (reg. 18, discussed in chapter 3). However, if a worker's employment is not in the transport sector but involves travel on the employer's behalf, then it seems likely that the time involved is 'working time'. It is therefore probable that the busy executive who is required to put in a morning's work at the office, then to catch a (subsonic) flight to New York and go straight into a lengthy business meeting will be entitled to count all that time towards the weekly average. The employer would be advised to work on that assumption and adjust hours in subsequent weeks or to seek agreement to an individual opt-out (assuming that the worker does not fall into the 'unmeasured working time' category). However, if the worker travels from Aberdeen to London on the employer's business and then spends the night in a hotel at the employer's expense, in order to carry out some duties the following day, it is submitted that the time spent at the hotel would not count as working time (unless the employee was required to work, have meetings etc.).

Training time

The draft Regulations only included time spent by young workers on training as 'working time'. This was wisely extended to all workers in the final version, for it would be odd if an employer was able to require workers to exceed time limits because they were being trained.

AGREEMENTS

The definition of 'working time' is just one of many areas under the Working Time Regulations 1998 where flexibility is provided for by allowing employers to reach alternative arrangements by agreement with their workers. It is thus convenient here to consider the kinds of agreement which can have effect to modify or exclude the Regulations. Under art. 17 of the Working Time Directive, various derogations are allowed 'by way of collective agreements or agreements concluded between the two sides of industry at the appropriate collective level'. The Labour government decided that its policy would be to take advantage of these so as to allow businesses and workers flexibility and freedom to organise working time as they wished (Consultation Document, para. 138). It may be questioned whether the procedures allowing derogations under the Working Time Regulations 1998 offer sufficient protection to workers before their rights are signed away. Derogations may be carried out by three kinds of agreement: collective agreements, workforce agreements and 'relevant agreements', as defined in reg. 2. In addition, an individual opt-out for the average 48-hour week is permitted.

Collective agreement

The following modifications or exclusions may be carried out by means of a collective agreement:

(a)   extension of the reference period for the average 48-hour week to 52 weeks (reg. 23(b));
(b)   night work limits (reg. 23(a));
(c)   entitlements to rest breaks (reg. 23(a), but see reg. 24).

By virtue of reg. 2, 'collective agreement' has the same meaning here as under the Trade Union and Labour Relations (Consolidation) Act 1992, s. 178; that is, 'any agreement or arrangement made by or on behalf of one or more trade unions and one or more employers or employers' associations and relating to one or more of the matters' specified in s. 178(2), which includes terms and conditions of employment. However, for the purposes of the Working Time Regulations 1998, only collective agreements made with *independent* trade unions will be acceptable. This will prevent exclusions being agreed with any company unions or staff associations which have not been able to persuade the Certification Officer of their freedom from possible interference by the employer in accordance with s. 5 of the 1992 Act.

Where employers recognise trade unions for collective bargaining, the resulting agreements bind all the workers in the bargaining unit, regardless of whether or not they are union members. Workers who are not union members therefore forgo the opportunity to make their voices heard in the negotiating process, despite the fact that the results may have an enormous impact on their terms and conditions. This has always been the case. However, the Working Time Regulations 1998 present something of a novelty in that it is the first time that collective agreements will actually be able to derogate from statutory employment protection rights. While unions and employers have long had the ability to contract out of the law on unfair dismissal by means of a dismissals procedure agreement, this is only possible where the agreement provides protection which is at least as good as the statutory protection (Employment Rights Act 1996, s. 110(3)(d)). Furthermore, only one such collective agreement has ever been concluded.

There is no requirement under the Trade Union and Labour Relations (Consolidation) Act 1992, s. 178, or the Regulations that collective agreements should be in writing. However, where they are intended to be used for the purposes of derogation, it is obviously prudent for them to be in written form. The Consultation Document suggested that a collective agreement covering these matters which preceded the Regulations could nevertheless be effective for derogation purposes. This is open to doubt. A worker could sensibly argue that any preceding collective agreement has been overtaken by the legislation and could not have been intended to have effect in these circumstances.

Workforce agreement

In *Commission of the EC* v *UK* (case C-383/92) [1994] ECR I-2479 the ECJ held that British implementation of the Collective Dismissals Directive (75/129/EEC) and the Acquired Rights Directive (77/187/EEC) was defective because, among other things, there were no provisions for consultation with employees where the employer did not recognise a trade union. The possibility for election of employee representatives for consultation purposes was therefore introduced by the Collective Redundancies and Transfer of Undertakings (Protection of Employment)

(Amendment) Regulations 1995. Although surviving a challenge on the grounds of continuing incompatibility with Community law in *R* v *Secretary of State for Trade and Industry, ex parte UNISON* [1996] ICR 1003, these regulations have been greatly criticised, in particular because of the lack of any stipulations as to the procedure and fairness of elections.

It was obvious that if the government wished to take advantage of the derogations permitted by the Working Time Directive, it would have to provide for a method of making agreements with employees without collective bargaining, since many employers do not recognise trade unions. On the other hand, the government was receptive to unions' arguments that where collective bargaining existed, it should not be undermined by allowing the employer to use an alternative means of making agreements with the workforce for this purpose. One of the unions' main grievances about the Collective Redundancies and Transfer of Undertakings (Protection of Employment) (Amendment) Regulations 1995 was that employers were allowed to consult with employee representatives even where a union was recognised. The government also accepted arguments that the procedures governing such agreements should be more tightly drawn than under those regulations. Hence the novel concept of the 'workforce agreement' was devised.

The conditions for a valid workforce agreement are set out in sch. 1 to the Working Time Regulations 1998. It can apply only to workers whose terms and conditions are not already covered, whether partly or wholly, by a collective agreement (sch. 1, para. 2), thus establishing the primacy of collective bargaining where there are recognised unions. To be valid, a workforce agreement must (a) be in writing, (b) have a defined term, which must not exceed five years, and (c) apply either to all workers (other than those covered by collective agreements) or to all such workers in a particular group which is defined by reference to its function, workplace, department or unit. It must also have been circulated before being made available for signing, together with 'such guidance as . . . workers might reasonably require in order to understand it fully' (sch. 1, paras 1 and 2).

It is the process for reaching agreement which has aroused most controversy. Usually, the agreement must be signed by the representatives of the relevant members of the workforce. However, if there are fewer than 20 workers employed in total by the employer, the individual agreement of the majority of the workers will suffice instead.

Employee representatives   Schedule 1, para. 3, stipulates that employee representatives must be elected by and from the relevant members of the workforce. It is left up to the employer to determine the number of representatives: the Regulatory Guidance, like Goldilocks, recommends that the number should be just right: 'sufficiently large to be representative of the workers concerned although not so large as to make negotiations unwieldy'. No relevant member of the workforce may be unreasonably excluded from standing for election, and all of them are entitled to vote. They must have as many votes as there are candidates, but there is no further stipulation, so presumably the election could either be first past the post or by transferable vote. The election must be conducted so as to secure that voting is in secret (so far as is reasonably practicable) and that votes are fairly and accurately counted. It is difficult to imagine situations where it would not be reasonably practicable to ensure secret voting.

The Regulations do not impose responsibility directly on the employer to ensure that these requirements are fulfilled, but clearly, if the employer wants to rely on the derogations, this will be necessary.

The rules for elections bear a passing resemblance to the rules applicable to trade unions for electing officials under the Trade Union and Labour Relations (Consolidation) Act 1992, but are much less prescriptive. This is one ground on which they have been criticised, for, it is argued, insufficient safeguards are provided. For example, there is no stipulation as to the minimum amount of time during which the draft agreement should be available to workers for consideration, nor even some formulation such as, 'long enough before the date of signature for workers reasonably to consider its terms' (compare the Transfer of Undertakings (Protection of Employment) Regulations 1981, reg. 10(2)). Secondly, it seems inappropriate to leave the employer with a free hand to determine the number of representatives. Thirdly, in sharp contrast to the legislation on trade union ballots, which requires fully postal ballots in all cases, the Working Time Regulations 1998 allow workplace ballots. If postal ballots are necessary to ensure that there is no ballot-rigging in union elections, the TUC argued that similar safeguards should have been included in these Regulations. Fourthly, in the absence of anything comparable to the Trade Union and Labour Relations (Consolidation) Act 1992, s. 48, which requires the circulation of election addresses, workers may be asked to elect representatives with no information about their position, length of service or opinions. There must be real questions as to whether such representatives will be genuinely independent and representative of the workforce.

There is no reason why employees who are representatives for the purposes of the Regulations should not also be representatives for consultation over redundancies and transfers of undertakings under the Collective Redundancies and Transfer of Undertakings (Protection of Employment) (Amendment) Regulations 1995 or for health and safety under the Health and Safety (Consultation with Employees) Regulations 1996, provided that the relevant rules for each set of regulations are followed and that it is clear to workers that they are electing representatives for all these purposes.

Majority agreement   It was originally proposed in the draft Regulations that a workforce agreement could always be entered into by getting the signature of a majority of the workforce. This was fiercely attacked by the TUC in their response to the Consultation Document as being incompatible with art. 17(3) of the Working Time Directive. They argued that the Directive only permits derogation where there is agreement between the two sides of industry, and that this requires a representative institution on both sides:

> This is nothing more than a statement of the principle that there is an inequality of bargaining power between employers and individual employees in a workplace and workers must act collectively if they are jointly to manage working time questions with the employer.

This is a powerful argument. It was accepted by the government to a large extent, in that the majority agreement option is now only available where there are fewer than 20 workers employed at the date on which the workforce agreement is signed.

However, it could be argued that this still allows improper pressure to be exerted on individuals and that there should be a secret ballot on whether to accept the agreement where the workforce is too small for a representative process.

It is also worth noting that the provision for agreement by a majority of the workers does not stipulate that these workers should also be covered by the agreement. It may have been assumed that with such a small workforce any agreement would cover all of them. This is not necessarily so. Suppose that the employer has a small factory workshop employing 12 workers and an office where three more are employed. The employer wishes to disapply the rest breaks for the factory workers only. It would seem from sch. 1, para. 1(d)(ii), as presently worded that the office workers would have a vote as well. If so, this would seem to be definitely incompatible with the Directive.

This highlights another problem: there is no easy way for workers to challenge a workforce agreement on the grounds of procedural defect. There are provisions in the Regulations and in the Employment Rights Act 1996 which protect workers from detriment or dismissal for asserting their rights under the Regulations or any other statutory rights (see below). However, the Regulations do not expressly give workers a *right* to have employee representatives or a properly run election. If a worker refused to accept a workforce agreement derogating from, say, his or her right to a rest break, and suffered a detriment or dismissal as a result, then these procedures would be available and could, in this indirect sense, be used to challenge the agreement's validity. But this is rather too late for the worker.

Where there is a valid workforce agreement, the following modifications or exclusions may be carried out:

(a) extension of the reference period for the average 48-hour week to 52 weeks (reg. 23(b));

(b) night work limits (reg. 23(a));

(c) entitlements to rest breaks (reg. 23(a), but see reg. 24).

Rights of worker representatives Workers who act as representatives for the purposes of negotiating workforce agreements and candidates for election as worker representatives receive statutory protection in connection with these activities. Regulations 31 and 32 insert new ss. 45A, 101A and 105A into the Employment Rights Act 1996 to provide them with a right not to suffer detriment, not to be dismissed and not to be selected for redundancy on grounds of performance of their functions. This protection parallels that given to employees who act as health and safety representatives (1996 Act, ss. 44 and 100), employee trustees of occupational pensions schemes (1996 Act, ss. 46 and 102) and employee representatives for consultation over redundancies or transfers of undertakings (1996 Act, ss. 47 and 103).

In the case of dismissal or selection for redundancy on these grounds, the dismissal is treated as automatically unfair and the usual conditions of a two-year qualifying period of continuous employment and exclusion of those over retiring age do not apply, (1996 Act, ss. 108, 109). Other special provisions are that the employee may have access to interim relief (1996 Act, s. 128), the basic award of compensation may not fall below a stipulated minimum (1996 Act, s. 120: £2,900 in 1998) and the employee will qualify for a special award if the employer refuses to comply with a re-employment order (1996 Act, s. 125).

The remedy of unfair dismissal is not open to worker representatives who are not 'employees' within the meaning of s. 230(1) of the 1996 Act: however, if their contracts were terminated because of their representative activities they could sue on the grounds that they had suffered a detriment, contrary to s. 45A of the 1996 Act. In these, circumstances, their only remedy will be compensation, which will be limited to the maximum compensation payable for unfair dismissal in a comparable situation (new s. 49(5A) of the 1996 Act, inserted by reg 31(3)).

While worker representatives under the Working Time Regulations 1998 will thus get the same protection as other statutory employee representatives, which is itself modelled on the protection of trade union members and officials under the Trade Union and Labour Relations (Consolidation) Act 1992, there is one significant difference. Whereas trade union officials and all the other statutory employee representatives have an express statutory right to time off with pay in order to carry out their functions, this has not been included in the Working Time Regulations 1998. It seems that a worker denied such facilities would have to attempt the indirect route of claiming for detriment if not permitted to take sufficient time for his or her duties.

Relevant agreements

A 'relevant agreement' is defined in reg. 2 as being one of three kinds of agreement: a collective agreement, a workforce agreement, or 'any other agreement in writing which is legally enforceable' between the parties. It thus comprises not only the two kinds of agreement described above, but also legally enforceable agreements between the employer and the individual worker, provided that they are in writing. This would apply to a written contract of employment, but not a written statement of particulars provided to an employee in accordance with the Employment Rights Act 1996, s. 1, since such a statement is evidence of a contract but is not itself an agreement in writing.

While some exclusions or modifications under the Regulations can be carried out only by collective agreement or workforce agreement, as indicated above, some matters can be dealt with by a legally enforceable individual agreement as an alternative. Examples include the definition of 'night time' (reg. 2) and commencement times for weekly rest and annual leave entitlements (regs 11(4) and 13(3)).

There is one other significant matter where individual agreement to exclude the Regulations is permitted. This is the opt-out from the 48-hour average weekly working hours limit, which is considered in the next section.

THE 48-HOUR AVERAGE WEEK

Perhaps the best known provision of the Working Time Regulations 1998 is the 48-hour limit on average weekly working time. One of the most important aims of the Working Time Directive as stated in the preamble was to ensure the safety and health of workers by placing a maximum limit on weekly working hours. This was fixed by art. 6 as an average of 48 hours a week, including overtime, and is implemented in regs 4 and 5 of the 1998 Regulations.

The reference period

Since the limit is on *average* weekly working hours, the critical issue is the length of the reference period over which the average is measured. The standard reference period is set at 17 weeks, which was considered to be the closest number of whole weeks to the four-month period stipulated in art. 16(2) of the Working Time Directive as the usual maximum. Regulation 4(3) provides that a relevant agreement may stipulate that the measurement should be over successive periods of 17 weeks; if not, the reference period is any period of 17 weeks during the worker's employment, effectively a rolling reference period. It will generally be in the employer's interest to reach agreement for consecutive periods, which will give more scope for dealing with varying needs.

For example, suppose that a worker normally has a 40-hour week and works just those normal hours for 11 weeks and then works 15 hours a week overtime for the next 6 weeks. This would amount to:

$$(11 \times 40 \text{ hours}) + (6 \times 55 \text{ hours}) = 770 \text{ hours} \tag{1}$$

This gives an average of 45.3 hours per week, which is within the limit.

But suppose that the need for overtime continues at a similar level for the next 10 weeks. If the rolling reference period is used, the worker could not be required to work the extra 15 hours throughout that time because, counting backwards from the end of the next 10 weeks, the worker's hours would be:

$$40 \text{ hours (week 1)} + 330 \text{ hours (weeks 2–7)} + 550 \text{ hours} = 920 \text{ hours} \tag{2}$$

This gives an average of 54.1 hours per week over a 17-week period, which is well outside the limit. However, if consecutive periods were used, the worker would be within the 48-hour limit for the first period, as we saw in (1) above. The employer could then require the worker to work the 15 hours overtime during the next 10 weeks and still remain within the 48-hour limit, provided that the hours were substantially reduced in the final seven weeks of the second period:

Period 2: $(10 \times 55 \text{ hours}) + (7 \times 38 \text{ hours }) = 816 \text{ hours}$ $\tag{3}$

This gives an average of 48 hours per week, and is thus not in breach of reg. 4. So provided the employer reduced the worker's hours to no more than 38 per week during the final seven weeks, there would be no breach of the Regulations.

This illustrates that consecutive reference periods allow the employer more scope for dealing with surges in need and also to plan so as not to exceed the limit.

Calculating the average

It is quite probable that during the reference period the employee may not work every day, for good reason. It would obviously be unreasonable to count these days in the calculation in order to reduce the overall average working hours. Thus reg. 4(7) provides that annual leave, sick leave, maternity leave and any time during which the individual opt-out was applicable are 'excluded days' for the purposes of the calculation. They are replaced by the equivalent number of days worked in the period immediately succeeding the end of the reference period.

Hence the calculation for average weekly working time is expressed in reg. 4(6) in the formula:

$$\frac{A + B}{C}$$

where A is the number of hours worked during the reference period, B is the number of hours worked immediately after the end of the reference period to make up for any excluded days, and C is the number of weeks in the reference period.

For example, suppose that consecutive reference periods have been agreed and that the worker, who has a standard 40-hour week, works 10 hours overtime a week in the first 10 weeks of the first period, then takes eight days as holiday, returning to work two 10-hour days and five more 40-hour weeks. The worker then works 10 hours overtime at the rate of two hours a day during what would normally be the first two weeks of the second period.

Expressed in terms of the formula in reg. 4(6), the worker's average hours are calculated as follows:

A (the hours worked in the reference period) = $(10 \times 50) + (2 \times 10) + (5 \times 40) = 720$
B (the extra hours in the immediately succeeding period making up for the excluded days) = $(8 \times 10) = 80$
C = 17

Therefore:

$$\frac{A + B}{C} = \frac{720 + 80}{17} = 47.1$$

which is within the limit.

It would seem that in a case such as this the second reference period in relation to the worker could still start immediately at the end of the first 17 weeks, notwithstanding that some of the days in the second period will also have been used in the calculation of average hours in the first period in relation to some individual workers, according to their personal circumstances. If this were not the case, the employer's duty to monitor and keep records of the hours worked in order to ensure compliance with the limits would be made much more difficult. The Regulations are silent on this point, so it would be prudent to deal with the question in the relevant agreement.

Extending the reference period

There are two situations where the reference period may be extended: (a) collective or workforce agreement, (b) for special categories of worker.

Collective or workforce agreement   According to reg. 23(b), the reference period can be extended to 52 weeks by a collective or workforce agreement 'for objective or technical reasons or reasons concerning the organisation of work'.

This suggests that employers and workers do not have a completely free hand in deciding on this extension, but quite what sort of limitation is meant by the reference to objective, technical or organisational reasons is far from clear. This is another example of the government opting simply to copy out the equivalent provision in the Working Time Directive (art. 17(4)) without speculating about what it might mean. The phrase is not dissimilar to the reference to 'economic, technical or organisational reasons entailing changes in the workforce' found in the Transfer of Undertakings (Protection of Employment) Regulations 1981, reg. 8, itself copied out of the Acquired Rights Directive (77/187/EEC), art. 4, but it seems unlikely that the case law on that provision will be helpful here. One interesting question will be whether the fact that the employer is willing to pay for this flexibility is sufficient.

Again, a dissident worker who is not satisfied that appropriate reasons exist for the extension of the reference period has no obvious way of challenging it. The Health and Safety Executive and the environmental health departments of local authorities are charged with enforcing the limits, but it seems hardly realistic to think that they would have the resources to intervene on such a complaint even if they had the power to do so. Ultimately the worker would probably have to assert his or her right to refuse to work more than the average by reference to a 17-week period and then take tribunal proceedings if any retaliatory action from the employer ensued — but this is hardly a satisfactory course of action.

The possibility of extending to 52 weeks means that annualised hours arrangements can continue. The Regulatory Guidance suggests that a collective agreement in force before 1 October 1998 could be effective for the purpose of extending the reference period, but it is submitted that this is doubtful. It would be wiser to ensure that an agreement directly referable to the Regulations is made.

Special cases   Regulation 4(5) provides that the reference period will be 26 weeks for the groups of workers identified as special cases in reg. 21. These special cases are discussed in chapter 3. Essentially, the derogation applies to kinds of work which either require continuous service (such as security, hospitals, telecommunications) or where external forces create unusual demands (such as seasonal needs in agriculture, tourism or to meet emergencies).

Temporary workers and new workers

Regulation 4(4) states that where a worker has worked for the employer for less than 17 weeks, the applicable reference period is the time since the beginning of the employment. This applies to new workers, but is particularly important for temporary workers. The government stated in its Consultation Document that it was important to give this protection to temporary workers 'who could otherwise find that it was lawful for their employer to require them to work longer than the limits envisaged by the Directive on the basis that they would do so only for the few weeks they are so employed and will leave before it is ever possible to determine a meaningful "17 week average"' (para. 60). Thus workers cannot be asked to work more than 48 hours during their first week, a total of 96 hours in the first two weeks, and so on.

Young workers

Under the Young Workers Directive, art. 8(2), young workers (there called 'adolescent workers') should not work more than eight hours a day and 40 hours a week. A limited derogation from this is allowed 'by way of exception or where there are objective grounds for so doing' (art. 8(5)). However, the UK was given a special dispensation by art. 17(1)(b) of that Directive not to implement this in the first four years after the date when the Directive was due to be implemented. The Young Workers Directive should have been implemented by 22 June 1996, so the UK's special exception lasts until 22 June 2000, at which stage there is due to be a report by the European Commission on the effect of this exemption and the Council will then decide whether to continue it or not.

Perhaps surprisingly, the government decided to take advantage of this derogation, stating its belief that the limits in the Working Time Directive give adequate protection for all workers. If this were so, it would hardly be the case that the EC would have made different and stricter provision in the Young Workers Directive than it did in the Working Time Directive. Furthermore, the individual opt-out is not restricted to adult workers, which means that young workers could agree to work far more than 48 hours a week. This can hardly be in their best interests, which could possibly affect the validity of such an agreement.

Unmeasured working time

The 48-hour limit does not apply to 'autonomous decision-takers' or self-managed executives as identified in reg. 20. The scope of this category is discussed in chapter 3. One difficult question for employers is to decide whether a senior worker falls into this category, in which case the limit does not apply, or whether the worker should be asked to agree to an opt-out. Simply stating in the contract that the worker is an autonomous decision-taker to whom the unmeasured working time derogation applies will not be sufficient, as this is not a matter to be settled by relevant agreement but by interpretation of the Regulations. However, framing the work and hours obligation in the contract so as to give genuine autonomy may suffice.

The individual opt-out

Article 18(1)(b) of the Working Time Directive controversially permitted Member States to have the option of disapplying the limit on working time subject to certain safeguards, in particular getting the individual's agreement. This is to be reviewed again by the time the Directive has been in force for seven years, i.e., by 23 November 2003.

The opt-out provision is made by the Working Time Regulations 1998, reg. 5, which lifts the limit where the worker has agreed to this in writing, whether for a specific period or indefinitely. The worker retains the right to terminate this concession at any time on giving appropriate notice. The notice period may be stipulated in the agreement, but may not be longer than three months (reg. 5(3)). If no notice period is stipulated, the worker need only give seven days' notice (reg. 5(2)(b)).

In addition, the employer must maintain up-to-date records relating to workers who have taken the opt-out. The records must identify the worker, set out any conditions relating to the agreement, and specify how many hours the worker has actually worked in each reference period since the agreement came into effect. If the agreement has lasted for more than two years, records need only be kept relating to the most recent two years. These records must be available for inspection by the HSE or local authority inspector, and the employer must be prepared to provide such further information as the inspector may request (reg. 5(4)).

It has been suggested that the level of record-keeping required for the opt-out is so onerous that it may not be worthwhile for the employer to seek this option. On the other hand, the employer may need to do so in respect of executive workers who regularly go over the limit because of the risk of otherwise committing an offence. The TUC was particularly critical of the opt-out provision, arguing that workers may find it difficult in practice to resist agreeing to opt out for fear that this will be regarded as a lack of commitment which will ultimately damage their employment prospects. Of course, workers have a remedy if they suffer a detriment or are dismissed for refusing to agree to an opt-out or if they terminate it, but they may well feel that in reality detriment will be difficult, if not impossible, to prove. The TUC also argued that 'it is contrary to general principles of health and safety law to allow people to "volunteer" to adopt an unsafe system of work'. It seems doubtful at present that working more than an average 48 hours a week is likely to be regarded as unsafe by the courts, although it is recognised that there comes a point at which excessive overtime is unsafe (*Johnstone* v *Bloomsbury Health Authority* [1992] QB 333). In so far as long working hours contribute to stress, employers must also be aware of their potential liability for their general duty of care towards their employees (cf. *Walker* v *Northumberland County Council* [1995] ICR 702).

Enforcement

Regulation 4(2) places a clear obligation on employers to enforce limits on working time. The employer must take 'all reasonable steps, in keeping with the need to protect the health and safety of workers,' to ensure that the limit is observed. By reg. 9, the employer has a further duty to keep, for a period of two years, records which are adequate to show compliance in respect of all workers covered by the Regulations. This is additional to the requirement already noted to keep specific records relating to workers who have agreed to the opt-out.

Failure to comply with any of these requirements is a criminal offence for which the employer could be liable for a fine of up to £5,000 on summary conviction, or an unlimited fine on indictment. One anxiety for employers is bound to be the level of record-keeping which is necessary for compliance with reg. 4, especially as this obligation potentially affects *all* employers, even if none of their workers usually works more than 48 hours per week. The Regulatory Guidance notes that, for hourly paid workers, the pay records alone would suffice. It further states that employers do not need to keep a running calculation of the average weekly working time of each worker and that if the standard contractual weekly working hours are clearly fewer than 48, it will be sufficient simply to have adequate systems to check that contractual hours are observed (para. 2.5). Clearly, employers do need to review their record-keeping systems in the light of the Regulations, to ensure compliance.

The Health and Safety Executive or local authority environmental health departments (for offices, shops, hotels and catering, sports and leisure facilities) have responsibility for enforcing these requirements. They have the same powers as under the Health and Safety at Work etc. Act 1974 to require production of records, to seek information and to enter premises for these purposes. This includes, in their repertoire of sanctions, the power to issue improvement notices or even prohibition notices. The big question is how rigorous enforcement will be in practice. The HSE has long been short of inspectors and there must be real doubts about whether it and local authorities are capable of dealing with the increased demands which the Working Time Regulations 1998 will place on them without substantially increased resources.

In addition to criminal sanctions there are civil remedies for workers if they suffer a detriment or are dismissed as a result, *inter alia*, of refusing to enter into, vary or extend any agreement with the employer as provided by the Regulations. As with worker representatives (see above) this is by virtue of new ss. 45A and 101A of the Employment Rights Act 1996, inserted by regs 31 and 32. Dismissal on these grounds is automatically unfair and there is no upper age limit or requirement of two years' continuous service (although the other special provisions for worker representatives do not apply). Workers who are not employees within the meaning of s. 230(1) of the 1996 Act cannot claim unfair dismissal in case of termination of their contracts, but could claim that they had suffered a detriment contrary to s. 45A of the 1996 Act. As with worker representatives, their compensation in these circumstances is limited to the comparable unfair dismissal maximum.

Workers with more than one job

The requirement in reg. 4(2) for an employer to take all reasonable steps to ensure that workers do not exceed the 48-hour average limit is not confined to those hours during which the worker is working for that particular employer. Thus, in the case of a worker with more than one job, the responsibility would seem to lie with each and every employer who employs him or her. The Regulatory Guidance suggests that an employer would have taken reasonable steps if either workers were asked if they had any other employment or were required under their contracts positively to reveal any other employment to the employer. In the event that the combination of two jobs means that the worker is over the limit, the employer is advised in the Regulatory Guidance to seek the worker's agreement. In general, an employer cannot forbid an employee to work for another employer in his or her free time, provided that confidential information is not at risk.

Chapter Five
Night Work and Shift Work

INTRODUCTION

Although there has never previously been a general statutory framework for the regulation of night work, which in the UK has been left to collective bargaining between employers and recognised trade unions, in the early part of the twentieth century legislation prohibited night work in industrial employment for women and young workers. These and other regulatory provisions were consolidated in the Factories Act 1961. The Sex Discrimination Act 1986 repealed restrictions on women's night work, and the Employment Act 1989 removed restrictions on the employment of young persons, while retaining controls in respect of children under the minimum school-leaving age.

The Directives require the regulation of night work and in particular a restriction on the hours of night work. Two key definitions apply to ascertain who is covered by these provisions as transposed by the Working Time Regulations 1998: 'night time' and 'night worker'.

Night time

Regulation 2(1) defines 'night time' as the period 11.00 p.m. to 6.00 a.m., or 'a period (a) the duration of which is not less than seven hours, and (b) which includes the period between midnight and 5.00 a.m.', which is determined by a 'relevant agreement' (i.e., a collective agreement, a workforce agreement, or other legally enforceable written agreement: see chapter 4).

Night worker

Regulation 2(1) defines 'night worker' as 'a worker (a) who, as a normal course, works at least three hours of his daily working time during night time, or (b) who is likely during night time, to work at least such proportion of his annual working time as may be specified for the purposes of these Regulations in a collective agreement or a workforce agreement'. This transposes art. 2(4) of the Working Time Directive. Regulation 2(1) provides that the first limb will be satisfied where the worker works 'three hours of his daily working time during night time' on the *majority* of days on which he works. However, this is 'without prejudice to the generality' of the expression 'as a normal course', which therefore implies that the expression 'as a normal course' does not necessarily require night work to be undertaken on the majority of working days. The Regulatory Guidance states that 'A worker may be said to work at night "as a normal course" if they do so on a regular basis, e.g. on a rotating shift pattern that resulted in them working regularly during night time, as opposed to on an infrequent or ad hoc basis' (para. 3.1.3). The second limb simply provides that a collective agreement or workforce agreement can confer the status of night worker on any worker who works a proportion of his or her annual working time during night time.

Young workers

Article 9 of the Young Workers Directive imposes a general prohibition on work by adolescent workers (i.e., workers over the minimum school-leaving age but under 18) either between 10.00 p.m. and 6.00 a.m. or 11.00 p.m. and 7.00 a.m., unless the adolescent is supervised by an adult, in which case a Member State can adopt measures to apply to specific activities, provided that the adolescent does not work between midnight and 4.00 a.m.. All Member States can derogate from these provisions in particular cases (e.g., for work performed in the shipping or fisheries sectors), provided there are objective grounds for doing so and the adolescent is provided with suitable compensatory rest time. Article 17(1)(b) grants the UK an opt-out from these provisions until 21 June 2000 with the possibility of further extension. The UK has taken advantage of this opt-out, and in the Working Time Regulations 1998 'night worker' includes both adult and adolescent workers unless the provision specifies otherwise. Although the Directive refers to adolescent workers and the Regulations refer to young workers the meaning is the same.

Under reg. 26, the special entitlements for young workers (e.g., under reg. 7(2), see below) do not apply to those working in the crew of seagoing vessels. The provisions of the Young Workers Directive which apply to this category of young worker have been implemented by the Merchant Shipping and Fishing Vessels (Health and Safety) (Employment of Chldren and Young Persons) Regulations 1998 (SI 1998/2411).

Overriding health and safety obligation

Article 1(4) of the Working Time Directive stipulates that 'the provisions of the Framework Health and Safety Directive 89/391/EEC are fully applicable to the matters referred to in paragraph 2, without prejudice to more stringent and/or specific provisions contained in this Directive'. The matters referred to in para. 2 include 'certain aspects of night work, shift work and patterns of work'. The preamble to the Young Workers Directive also makes reference to the Framework Directive.

The implication is that in interpreting the Working Time Directive (and as a corollary the Young Workers Directive) the ECJ will recognise the ongoing duty of the employer to assess risks in order to prevent harm to the health and safety of workers. The Young Workers Directive explicitly imposes general and specific health and safety obligations on the employers of, *inter alia*, young workers (arts

6 and 7). Since the Regulations have been enacted in order to implement the Directives, UK courts will comply with their obligation under *Marleasing SA v La Comercial Internacional de Alimentación SA* (case C-106/89) [1990] ECR I-4135 to interpret the Regulations consistently with the Directives, even if this requires distorting the meaning of the Regulations (see chapter 2).

LENGTH OF NIGHT WORK

Article 8(1) of the Working Time Directive requires particular limits to apply to 'normal hours of work for night workers'. Article 8(2) imposes a stricter limit on 'night workers whose work involves special hazards or heavy physical or mental strain'.

Regulation 6 of the Working Time Regulations 1998 requires an employer to 'take all reasonable steps, in keeping with the need to protect the health and safety of workers, to ensure that' the 'normal' hours of work of a night worker do not exceed the limit of an average of eight in any 24-hour period. This limit applies equally to adult and young workers, since the UK has taken advantage of its opt-out in respect of young workers, as discussed above. Article 8(1) of the Working Time Directive appears to be stricter in that it requires Member States to take the necessary measures to ensure that 'normal hours of work for night workers do not exceed an average of eight hours in any 24-hour period', and there is no provision for an employer to argue that 'all reasonable steps' have been taken to ensure that the hours of the night worker do not exceed this limit.

The reference period

Regulation 6 provides for a night worker's average 'normal hours of work' to be calculated over a reference period of 17 weeks. This is the same reference period as is used for the calculation of weekly working time under reg. 4. In setting this reference period, art. 16(3) of the Working Time Directive required Member States to consult the two sides of industry. In response to the Consultation Document issued by the previous Conservative government, trade unions and trade union bodies generally argued for a 24-hour limit unless varied by a collective agreement. The TUC suggested that in these circumstances there could be a maximum reference period of three months. The National Union of Journalists, whose members would be particularly affected by the provisions, suggested that if there was to be a reference period then it should be four months (i.e., the same as for the weekly working time limit under reg. 4). Employers and employers' organisations generally favoured a standard reference period of over six months and up to one year. However, the CBI proposed a four-month standard reference period, which could be extended to six or 12 months where derogations applied. Among other bodies responding, the Institute of Personnel and Development proposed 12 months, and the Manchester Low Pay Unit two weeks. In selecting the 17-week period as the standard reference period, the present government states that it has taken into account the views expressed on this issue in response to the Conservative government's Consultation Document (Consultation Document URN 98/645, para. 70).

As with the limit on weekly working time, the 17-week reference period can either be successive periods of 17 weeks as specified in a relevant agreement or any 17 weeks during the worker's employment — a rolling reference period (reg. 6(3)). From the point of view of an employer, successive periods with a common starting date for all workers is a better option, for the reasons indicated in chapter 4. This will also make record-keeping obligations easier, especially since the employer can use the same reference period for night work as is used for measuring working time.

Calculating the average normal hours of work

Regulation 6(5) sets out the formula to be applied to calculate a night worker's average normal hours of work for each 24 hours during the 17-week reference period:

$$\frac{A}{B - C}$$

where A is the number of hours during the reference period which are the normal working hours for that worker; B is the number of days during the reference period; and C is the total number of hours during the reference period comprised in rest periods spent by the worker in pursuance of the entitlement under reg. 11 (weekly rest periods), divided by 24.

   If, during the first 17-week reference period a night worker's normal working hours consist of five nine-hour periods in each seven-day period, the total number of normal working hours over the 17-week reference period is $17(5 \times 9) = 765$. There are 119 days during the 17-week reference period (i.e., 17×7 days) and the worker is entitled to 17 24-hour rest periods under reg. 11. The worker's average normal hours of work for each 24-hour period is therefore $765 \div (119 - 17) = 765 \div 102 = 7.5$ and the limit is therefore observed.

Temporary workers and new workers

Special provisions apply where a night worker has worked for the employer for less than 17 weeks. In this situation, reg. 6(4) provides that the worker's average normal hours of work will be calculated by reference to the period since the worker started work for the employer. Therefore, a night worker who starts work on 12 October 1998 must not have normal hours of work of more than eight hours during the first 24-hour period, a total of 16 hours during the first 48-hour period, and so on. Once the worker becomes entitled to a 24-hour weekly rest period under reg. 11, that will have to be discounted from the calculation, in accordance with the formula set out in reg. 6(5) (see above). Regulation 6(4) does not allow a newly employed night worker to undertake normal working hours consisting of, for example, five nine-hour periods during the first week of employment; however, this will be possible at a later stage during the initial 17-week period.

   To give an example, if in week 1 a night worker's normal working hours consist of five eight-hour periods, the average normal hours of work for the week will be $40 \div (7 - 1) = 40 \div 6 = 6.7$ hours. If in week 2, the employer amends the normal working hours to consist of five nine-hour periods, the average will then be $(40 + 45) \div (14 - 2) = 85 \div 12 = 7.1$ hours, which would still be within the prescribed limit.

The government believes that this provision is necessary:

in order to protect and secure the rights of 'temporary' workers, who could otherwise find that it was lawful for their employer to require them to work longer than the limits envisaged by the Directive on the basis that they would do so only for the few weeks they are so employed and will leave before it would be possible to determine a '17 week average' (Consultation Document URN 98/645, para. 73).

Normal working hours

Under reg. 6, the limit is on the worker's 'normal hours of work' rather than the hours *actually* worked and the Regulatory Guidance states that it is therefore irrelevant if the worker is absent due to illness (para. 3.1.6). This should be contrasted with reg. 4, which, in the context of maximum weekly working time, aggregates the total hours *actually* worked during the applicable reference period to ascertain if the limit has been exceeded (see Chapter 4, above).

There is an obligation under the Employment Rights Act 1996, s. 1, to provide employees with a statement of their particulars of employment within two months of the start of their employment. Section 1(4)(c) provides that this statement should contain particulars of 'any terms and conditions relating to hours of work (including any terms and conditions relating to *normal working hours*)' (emphasis added).

Regulation 6(6) of the Working Time Regulations 1998 provides that if the Employment Rights Act 1996, s. 234, applies to a worker, the worker's 'normal hours of work' are the worker's 'normal working hours' as defined by the 1996 Act. Section 234 provides that:

(1)   Where an employee is entitled to overtime pay when employed for more than a fixed number of hours in a week or other period, there are for the purposes of this Act normal working hours in his case.

(2)   Subject to subsection (3), the normal working hours in such a case are the fixed number of hours.

(3)   Where in such a case—
   (a)   the contract of employment fixes the number, or minimum number, of hours of employment in a week or other period (whether or not it also provides for the reduction of that number or minimum in certain circumstances), and
   (b)   that number or minimum number of hours exceeds the number of hours without overtime,
the normal working hours are that number or minimum number of hours (and not the number of hours without overtime).

Section 234 applies to employees (rather than workers, which has a broader scope: see chapter 3) who are entitled to overtime pay when employed for more than a fixed number of hours in a week or other period. In this case, the normal working hours are the fixed number of hours (i.e., overtime actually worked is excluded). Therefore, if a contract of employment provides that the employee will work 40 hours per week at £5 per hour, after which overtime rates will apply at £7 per hour, then the normal working hours will be 40, even if the employee actually works 60 hours in a week. However, if the contract of employment fixes the number, or a minimum number, of hours of employment in a week or other period and that number of hours exceeds the number of hours without overtime, then the normal working hours are that number, and not the number of hours without overtime. For example, if the contract provides that the employee will work 50 hours per week (or at least 50 hours per week) and overtime rates at time and a half will apply to hours in excess of 40 hours, normal working hours will be 50.

Thus normal working hours will not include overtime unless there is a contractual obligation on both parties to the agreement, i.e., on the employer to provide the overtime and on the employee to work the overtime. This was confirmed by the Court of Appeal in *Tarmac Roadstone Holdings Ltd* v *Peacock* [1973] ICR 273, which was followed by the Court of Appeal in *Lotus Cars Ltd* v *Sutcliffe* [1982] IRLR 381. In *Tarmac Roadstone*, the contract provided for a fixed period of 40 hours per week. Employees were obliged to work overtime if required by the employer, but there was no obligation on the employer to provide overtime. The Court of Appeal held that the employee's normal working hours were 40 per week even though he regularly worked 57 hours per week. This is confirmed in the Regulatory Guidance, which states that:

> Where a worker works overtime, their normal working hours are the hours of work fixed by their contract of employment. Time worked as overtime is not normal working time unless a worker's contract fixes a minimum number of hours, including overtime, which is more than their notional fixed hours (para. 3.1.6).

This being the case, there would appear to a major conflict with the Working Time Directive. The aim of the Directive is to provide a further safeguard to night workers, over and above that under art. 6. This is clearly set out in the preamble to the Directive:

> Whereas research has shown that the human body is more sensitive at night to environmental disturbances and also to certain burdensome forms of work organisation and that long periods of night work can be detrimental to the health of workers and can endanger safety at the workplace;
>   Whereas there is a need to limit the duration of periods of night work, *including overtime* . . . (emphasis added).

This has not been reflected in the Regulations, as the definition of normal working hours excludes most overtime. It could be argued that the difference in wording between reg. 4 and reg. 6 is justified by the Working Time Directive itself, in that art. 6 (maximum weekly working time) refers to 'average working time', whereas art. 8 (length of night work) refers to 'normal hours of work'. However, the term 'normal hours of work' has a technical meaning in English law which does not exist in EC law, and it is submitted that transposing art. 8 so as to include this technical meaning is inconsistent with the terms of the Directive.

Given that the preamble actually refers to imposing limits on the duration of night work, including overtime, it appears incongruous that overtime actually worked may not be taken into account when calculating 'normal working hours' under reg. 6. This would mean that a night worker who regularly did an hour's overtime on top of an eight-hour night shift throughout the reference period, because required to do so by the employer, would not be over the night work limit despite regularly working nine hours a night.

If this constitutes inadequate implementation of the Directive, then there are two options available, as explained in chapter 2. The first option is available to workers who are employed by the State or an emanation of the State: provided the provision in question is sufficiently clear and precise as to be capable of direct enforcement, then the employee can rely upon the Directive rather than the Regulations. If the provision does not satisfy this test, or if the worker is not employed by the State or its emanation, then the principle of indirect effect requires national courts and tribunals to interpret national law in a way which is compatible with the Directive, wherever that is possible. It would, however, be difficult for a lower court or tribunal faced with the question to define normal working hours differently from what is now established precedent in the Court of Appeal, especially as the inconsistency with the terms of the Directive is not absolutely clear-cut. In these circumstances, a reference to the ECJ in accordance with art. 177 EC Treaty [art. 234] to clarify the meaning of the Directive and the adequacy of the implementing Regulations would seem to be inevitable.

The other provisions in the Regulations relating to, *inter alia*, maximum weekly working time, daily and weekly rest periods and rest breaks also apply to night workers.

Special hazards and heavy physical or mental strain

Regulation 6(7), which transposes art. 8(2) of the Working Time Directive, provides that an employer shall ensure that no night worker whose work involves 'special hazards or heavy physical or mental strain works for more than eight hours in any 24-hour period during which the night worker performs night work'. This is a complete bar, and there is no watering down of the provision with wording such as 'an employer shall take all reasonable steps to ensure that . . .' as is found in reg. 6(2). There is no averaging over a 17-week reference period; if the work of a night worker involves special hazards or heavy physical or mental strain, then the employer must ensure that the worker does not *actually* work more than eight hours in any 24-hour period. Regulation 6(8) provides that the work of a night worker shall be regarded as involving special hazards or heavy physical or mental strain if it is identified as such in a collective agreement or a workforce agreement which takes account of the specific effects and hazards of night work, or if it is recognised in a risk assessment made by the employer under the Management of Health and Safety at Work Regulations 1992 (SI 1992/2051 as amended by SI 1994/2865 and SI 1997/135), reg. 3, as involving a significant risk to the health and safety of workers. Neither the Directive nor the Regulations stipulate that it is of any relevance how much of a night worker's work involves special hazards or heavy physical or mental strain. The government states that 'The presumption may be, therefore, that if *any* of a night worker's work is in that category, the absolute limit of no more than eight hours work in any period of 24 hours in which they do any night work applies' (Consultation Document URN 98/645, para. 78).

Derogations

Regulation 19 provides that the restrictions on length of night work contained in reg. 6(1), (2) and (7) do not apply in relation to an adult or young worker employed as a domestic servant in a private household, e.g., an au pair or nanny.

Regulations 20 and 21 also apply to exclude these provisions in relation to a worker where the duration of the working time is not measured or predetermined or can be determined by the worker; or to other special cases (see chapter 3). Regulation 23 provides for a collective agreement or workforce agreement to modify or exclude these provisions (see chapter 4). Regulation 24 requires that where these provisions are modified or excluded under regs 21 or 23 so that the night worker is required to work during a period which would otherwise be a rest period, then:

(a)   his employer shall wherever possible allow him to take an equivalent period of compensatory rest, and

(b)   in exceptional cases in which it is not possible, for objective reasons, to grant such a period of rest, his employer shall afford him such protection as may be appropriate in order to safeguard the worker's health and safety.

The Regulatory Guidance states that 'An equivalent period of rest should be considered to be a period of rest as long as that which the worker was entitled to but not able to take' (para. 3.2.4). Although the Regulations are silent on this matter, the Guidance continues: 'Compensatory rest should be provided within a reasonable time from when the entitlement to rest was modified' (para. 3.2.4). These are matters which could usefully be dealt with by collective or workforce agreement.

Enforcement

Enforcement of reg. 6(2) and (7) is the responsibility of the Health and Safety Executive, which has a duty to 'make adequate arrangements for the enforcement' of these provisions (reg. 28(2)). It is provided in reg. 28(3) and (4) that where a local authority has been given the responsibility under the Health and Safety (Enforcing Authority) Regulations 1998 (SI 1998/494) in relation to workers employed in certain premises, then that local authority, through its environmental health officers, is under a duty to enforce these provisions, and it shall do so in accordance with any guidance issued by the Health and Safety Commission. The Health and Safety Executive is responsible for factories, building sites, mines, farms, fairgrounds, quarries, chemical plants, nuclear installations, schools and hospitals. Local authority environmental health officers are responsible for retailing, offices, hotels and catering, sports, leisure and consumer services.

Enforcement of current health and safety law is undertaken by Health and Safety Executive inspectors or local authority environmental health officers and therefore it is a tried and tested method of enforcement which is carried out in accordance with 'good practice principles' which the government states 'currently mean that enforcing officials will explain to an employer any suggestions for remedial action and offer the employer the right to make representations before commencing any legal action against the employer' (Consultation Document URN 98/645, para. 175). The government expects the enforcement officers to make the same arrangements in respect of the enforcement of reg. 6(2) and (7). The government states that:

Advice and warnings would usually precede any more formal action, such as the issue of a notice requiring changes within a specified period of time. Notices can, however, be an effective and quick means of getting employers to take necessary corrective action without delay, and without the disruption and inconvenience of having to go to court. Appeals against a notice can be made by an employer to an employment tribunal (Consultation Document URN 98/645 para. 176).

The Regulatory Guidance states that enforcement 'will be in line with the Health and Safety Commission's Enforcement Policy Statement' (para. 3.4).

Regulation 28(5) provides that certain provisions of the Health and Safety at Work etc. Act 1974 which are relevant to enforcement will apply to the enforcement of these provisions, in particular certain provisions of s. 20, which empower inspectors, *inter alia*, to enter premises, and ss. 21 and 22, which provide for the service of improvement notices and prohibition notices.

Ultimately, reg. 29 makes it a criminal offence for an employer to fail to comply with these provisions, or, *inter alia*, to contravene any requirement or prohibition imposed by an improvement notice or a prohibition notice which has been issued under ss. 21 or 22 respectively of the Health and Safety at Work etc. Act 1974. The government has stated that it expects the enforcement officers to proceed informally or through the issuing of an improvement or prohibition notice before instituting criminal proceedings. This would obviously depend upon the gravity of the breach and its consequences.

Regulations 31 and 32 insert new ss. 45A, 101A and 105(4A) into the Employment Rights Act 1996 giving workers a right not to be subjected to any detriment, not to be dismissed and not to be selected for redundancy for, *inter alia*, refusing to enter into, vary or extend an agreement to modify the Regulations, or to comply with a requirement of the employer which would be in breach of the Regulations. For example, if the employer took retaliatory action against a worker who refused to enter a workforce agreement to extend the reference period for measuring night work or who indicated an unwillingness to work beyond the statutory limits on night work, the worker would be able to make a complaint to an employment tribunal. The usual three-month limitation period applies, but there is no requirement for a period of continuous service and the upper age limit exclusion for unfair dismissal does not apply.

It is worth noting that the right in new s. 45A of the Employment Rights Act 1996 not to be subjected to any detriment applies whether the detriment consists of a positive action 'or any deliberate failure to act . . .' This formulation avoids the problem thrown up by the House of Lords' decision in *Associated Newspapers* v *Wilson/Associated British Ports* v *Palmer* [1995] IRLR 259 in relation to the otherwise comparable right to claim for action short of dismissal on union membership grounds (TURLCA s. 146). In the joined appeals in *Wilson/Palmer* the House of Lords held that 'action short of dismissal' did not include an omission on the part of an employer to offer a benefit to one group of employees on union membership grounds. A deliberate failure to give a pay increase to workers who refuse to agree to work beyond any of the working time limits would constitute a detriment under s. 45A. It is unclear whether a threat of detriment by an employer would be sufficient for a worker to bring a claim.

There is no statutory limit on the amount of compensation which can be awarded under s. 45A, although the limits for unfair dismissal apply to actions under ss. 101A and 105A. It is therefore provided that where the complainant is an employee, he or she cannot claim for detriment unless the contract is for a fixed term and a waiver clause has been signed (s. 45A(4)). If the contract of a worker who is not an 'employee' within the meaning of s. 230(1) of the Employment Rights Act 1996 is terminated, the only possible claim is for detriment contrary to s. 45A, but in this situation new s. 49(5A) stipulates that the amount of compensation may not exceed the amount which would have been payable had it been an unfair dismissal claim.

It is possible, however, that the limit on dismissal compensation could breach the Community law principle which provides that remedies must be effective so as to protect an individual's Community law rights (see, for example, *Marshall* v *Southampton and South West Hampshire Health Authority (Teaching) (No. 2)* (case C-271/91) [1993] ECR I-4367).

This issue is currently under review by the government. In its White Paper, *Fairness at Work* (Cm 3968), the government stated its intention to abolish the limit on compensatory awards in unfair dismissal cases (para. 3.5) although it now seems likely that the limit may remain but be raised to a significantly higher level, perhaps £50,000.

Regulation 35 provides that any provision in an agreement which purports to exclude or limit the operation of any provision of the Regulations, or preclude a person from making a complaint to a tribunal is void, unless an ACAS conciliation officer has taken action under the Employment Tribunals Act 1996, s. 18, or the parties have signed a compromise agreement which complies with the requirements set out in reg. 35(3).

Records

Regulation 9 requires employers to keep records which are adequate to ensure that the limits specified in, *inter alia*, reg. 6(1) and (7) are being complied with and to keep such records for two years from the date on which they were made. There is no prescribed form for the records, but employers will need to show how they have complied with this requirement.

Regulation 25 provides that reg. 9 does not apply in relation to a worker (young or adult) serving as a member of the armed forces (i.e., any of the naval, military and air forces of the Crown: reg. 2(1)).

HEALTH ASSESSMENT FOR NIGHT WORKERS

Regulation 7(1) requires an employer to provide an adult worker with the opportunity of a free health assessment before being assigned to night work, unless the worker has previously had a health assessment and the employer has no reason to believe that that assessment is no longer valid. The employer is also required to ensure that each night worker has the opportunity of a free health assessment 'at regular intervals of whatever duration may be appropriate in his case'. This transposes part of art. 9 of the Working Time Directive.

In the case of young workers employed during the period 10.00 p.m. and 6.00 a.m., reg. 7(2) imposes a similar obligation, but rather than a 'free health assessment' the young worker is to be given the opportunity of a 'free assessment of his health and capacities'. The employer is also required to ensure that each young worker has the opportunity of a free health and capacities assessment 'at regular intervals of whatever duration may be appropriate in his case'. Regulation 7(2) does not apply where the work that the young worker is assigned to 'is of an exceptional nature' (reg. 7(4)). This transposes part of art. 9(3) of the Young Workers Directive.

The purpose of the initial health assessment is to ascertain whether the worker is fit to undertake the night work to which the worker is to be assigned. A number of medical conditions may in some cases be made worse by working at night. The Regulatory Guidance gives a non-exhaustive list of examples (para. 4.1.2):

(a)   diabetes, particularly where treatment with insulin injections on a strict timetable is required,

(b)   some heart and circulatory disorders, particularly where factors such as physical stamina are affected,

(c)   stomach or intestinal disorders, such as ulcers, and conditions where the timing of a meal is particularly important,

(d)   medical conditions affecting sleep,

(e)   some chronic chest disorders where night-time symptoms may be particularly troublesome,

(f)   other medical conditions requiring regular medication on a strict timetable.

The additional requirement in the case of young workers employed during the period 10.00 p.m. and 6.00 a.m. is to a health 'and capacities' assessment which by implication should be more wide-ranging than the corresponding assessment for adult night workers. The government states that such an assessment would need to consider the young worker's 'physical and psychological abilities to undertake the night work to which he is assigned' (Consultation Document URN 98/645, para. 81). The Regulatory Guidance states that such an assessment will need to consider issues like 'physique, maturity and experience, and take into account competence to undertake the night work that has been assigned' (para 4.3).

For both an adult and a young night worker there must be reassessment at 'regular intervals of whatever duration may be appropriate in his case' (reg. 7(1) and (2)). There is no attempt to specify maximum or minimum intervals between assessments. In its Consultation Document the government stated that:

the range of types of work and the capacities of individuals make it inappropriate and impracticable to contemplate laying down mandatory rules which would impose maximum limits on the time between assessments. For the same reasons, it would be wrong to specify a certain minimum period between assessment (para. 82).

The Regulatory Guidance states that:

> The frequency of repeat assessments will vary between individuals according to factors such as the type of night work, its duration and the age and health of the individual worker. Where appropriate, the employer should be guided by the judgment of a health care professional. As a rule of thumb, it would be prudent for repeat screening questionnaires to be completed annually (para. 4.1.3).

Neither the Directives nor the Regulations refer to a 'medical' assessment, and therefore the government considers that the assessment would not initially have to be undertaken by a qualified medical practitioner: 'a well designed questionnaire could be used in the first instance to identify individuals whose health might be harmed by night work' (Consultation Document, para. 84). However, the Regulatory Guidance states that if a screening questionnaire is adopted it 'should be compiled with guidance from a qualified health care professional such as a doctor or nurse familiar with the employer's business and the issues associated with working at night' (para 4.1.2). The Guidance advises that the questionnaire should explain its purpose to the worker, the nature of the work to which the worker has been assigned, and ask whether the worker suffers from any medical condition or is undergoing any medical treatment (such as the examples listed above) which might affect the worker's fitness to work at night.

Screening of the questionnaires should be undertaken by people with appropriate training to interpret the information. Any individual identified with conditions which might be affected by working at night could then be referred to a qualified health professional for further assessment (e.g., to an employer's occupational health officer or a GP). However, because of the special nature of a young worker, and bearing in mind that only the UK has an opt-out from the general prohibition on young workers undertaking night work, a 'well designed questionnaire' may not be suitable to satisfy this requirement.

Regulation 7(3) provides that an assessment under reg. 7(1) or (2) is free 'if it is at no cost to the worker to whom it relates'. The government states that 'the employer would be liable to pay for any relevant charge from the body or person carrying out the assessment, and the worker should not have to lose wages or incur other expenses because of having an assessment carried out' (Consultation Document URN 98/645, para. 80). This is also confirmed in the Regulatory Guidance (para. 4.1).

The assessment is confidential and can only be disclosed to any person other than the worker if either the worker consents to this in writing or where the disclosure simply amounts to a statement that the worker is fit to perform night work (reg. 7(5)). The Regulatory Guidance states that:

> Two types of information arise from the health assessment. A simple fitness-for-work statement should be provided by the health care professional to the employer. Clinical information, however, must remain confidential and can only be released to an employer (or any third party) with the worker's consent. Screening questionnaires containing non-clinical information can be stored with an individual's personnel record (para. 4.1.2).

Derogations

Workers (adult or young) who are employed as domestic servants in a private household, e.g., a nanny or au pair, are excluded by reg. 19 from the provisions on health assessments for night workers.

Enforcement

Failure by an employer to comply with the health assessment provisions is a criminal offence, whose enforcement is the responsibility of health and safety enforcement officers as already described.

The Consultation Document (URN 98/645, p. 58) indicates that there is no right of individual complaint to an employment tribunal where the employer fails in its duty to carry out health assessments. However, it is quite possible that the new ss. 45A and 101A and the amended s. 105 of the Employment Rights Act 1996, discussed above, will apply. Section 45A provides that a worker has the right not to be subjected to any detriment imposed by the employer because the worker has, *inter alia*, refused (or proposed to refuse) to comply with a requirement which the employer imposed (or proposed to impose) in contravention of the employer's obligations under the Regulations. Under reg. 7(1) the employer is under an obligation not to assign an adult worker to night work unless he or she is provided with the opportunity of a free health assessment. Therefore, an adult worker denied promotion, for example, for refusing to work nights until the employer had complied with this obligation, will have suffered a detriment; this would apply equally to the employer's obligation to young workers under reg. 7(2).

By the same token, dismissal or selection for redundancy in these circumstances would be covered by ss. 101A and 105(4A) of the 1996 Act.

If this is not correct, then an employee (in the narrow sense) who has been dismissed would at least have the right to make a complaint of unfair dismissal pursuant to s. 94 of the 1996 Act, provided that he or she met the qualifying conditions (e.g., length of service, upper age limit), but the dismissal would not be automatically unfair. The tribunal would have to decide whether the dismissal was fair or unfair in accordance with the reasonableness standard in s. 98(4).

Records

Regulation 9 requires employers to keep records which are adequate to ensure that the limits specified in, *inter alia*, reg. 7(1) and (2) are being complied with and to keep such records for two years from the date on which they were made. There is no prescribed form for the records, but employers will need to show how they have complied with this requirement.

Regulation 25 provides that reg. 9 does not apply in relation to a worker (young or adult) serving as a member of the armed forces (i.e., any of the naval, military and air forces of the Crown: reg. 2(1)).

TRANSFER TO DAY WORK

Regulation 7(6) provides that if a registered general practitioner advises an employer that a night worker is suffering from health problems which the practitioner considers to be connected with the fact that the worker performs night work, and 'it is possible for the employer to transfer the worker' to work to which the worker is suited and which removes the worker from the scope of night work, then 'the employer shall transfer the worker accordingly'. This transposes art. 9(1)(b) of the Working Time Directive. The Regulatory Guidance states that if a worker's fitness for night work becomes affected by a disability an employer has a *duty* under the Disability Discrimination Act 1995 to make reasonable adjustments:

> which might include changes to the worker's hours of work. The purpose of this is to overcome any disadvantage to the worker because of their disability and arising from a requirement to undertake night work (para. 4.1.4).

The Guidance also states that special considerations should be given to new and expectant mothers, and young workers. The only exclusion from the obligation to transfer to day work relates to a worker (adult or young) who is employed as a domestic servant in a private household (reg. 17). As with the duty to carry out health assessments, enforcement is primarily in the hands of health and safety enforcement officers backed up by criminal sanctions.

Although the government's Consultation Document indicates that there is no right of individual complaint to an employment tribunal, the same line of argument as for health assessments is applicable here. Thus, it may be possible to make a complaint under ss. 45A, 101A or 105 of the Employment Rights Act 1996, or if this were deemed not to be possible, and an employee (in the narrow sense) has been dismissed, a complaint could be made under the general law of unfair dismissal, pursuant to s. 94 of the 1996 Act.

SAFETY AND HEALTH PROTECTION FOR NIGHT WORKERS AND SHIFT WORKERS

Article 12 of the Working Time Directive requires Member States to take the measures necessary to ensure that night workers and shift workers 'have safety and health protection appropriate to the nature of their work'; and that 'appropriate protection and prevention services or facilities with regard to the safety and health of night workers and shift workers are equivalent to those applicable to other workers and are available at all times'. The government considers that these obligations have already been given effect through the Management of Health and Safety at Work Regulations 1992 (SI 1992/2051):

> Those regulations require employers to ensure that appropriate protection and prevention services are made available for workers in general. Those regulations make no distinction as to time of the day, therefore it is the government's view that those regulations apply equally to both 'day' and 'night' workers and that their requirements provide sufficient and appropriate protection for all workers (Consultation Document URN 98/645, para. 89).

Whether or not the government's view is correct remains to be seen. Under reg. 3 of the Management of Health and Safety at Work Regulations 1992, an employer is under an obligation to undertake a risk assessment in respect of the health and safety of employees. Enforcement of these provisions is through the Health and Safety enforcement agencies; there is no right for an individual to make a complaint to an employment tribunal, because art. 12 has not been transposed into the Regulations.

The requirement of art. 12 that employers provide 'equivalent' appropriate protection and prevention services or facilities could be problematic, despite what the government states. What is to be regarded as 'equivalent' is not further defined in the Directive. It could mean, for example, that if an employer provided a nurse or doctor on site during daytime (e.g., 9.00 a.m. to 5.00 p.m.), then this service would also have to be provided during shifts or at night. This concept of equivalence will have to be resolved ultimately by the ECJ, but since there is no individual method of enforcement in the UK it may take time before this is challenged. This could come about by, for example, a trade union making an application for judicial review seeking a declaration that this provision of the Directive has not been adequately transposed by the UK.

Chapter Six
Rest Breaks and Rest Periods

INTRODUCTION

As with limits on working time, there was no general statutory framework stipulating that workers should be allowed rest breaks until the introduction of the Working Time Regulations 1998, although at different times there has been legislation for specific groups of workers (e.g., children, women) or sectors (e.g., shop workers). With the limited exception of agricultural workers, miners, sheet glass workers and some transport drivers, all statutory measures regulating working time were repealed during the 1980s and 1990s when successive Conservative governments pursued employment deregulation policies. Implementation of the Directives therefore represents a new chapter in the development of labour law in the UK.

The Working Time and Young Workers Directives provide workers with entitlements for daily and weekly rest periods and a daily break. With regard to adult workers generally, art. 3 of the Working Time Directive provides that 'every worker is entitled to a minimum daily rest period of 11 consecutive hours per 24-hour period'. Article 5 provides that 'per each seven-day period, every worker is entitled to a minimum uninterrupted rest period of 24 hours plus the eleven hours' daily rest referred to in Article 3'. Article 4 provides that 'where the working day is longer than six hours, every worker is entitled to a rest break'. More generous entitlements are provided to adolescent workers (i.e., workers over the minimum school leaving age but under 18) under the Young Workers Directive.

These provisions have been transposed into UK law by the Working Time Regulations 1998 in almost identical language to that used in the Directive, although, instead of 'adolescent workers' the Regulations refer to 'young workers', which has the same meaning.

Under reg. 26 the special entitlements for young workers (e.g., under regs 10(2), 11(3) and 12(4)) do not apply to those working in the crew of seagoing vessels. Those provisions of the Young Workers Directive which apply to this category of young worker have been transposed by the Merchant Shipping and Fishing Vessels (Health and Safety) (Employment of Children and Young Persons) Regulations 1998 (SI 1998/2411) which came into force on 30 October 1998.

Overriding health and safety obligation

Article 1(4) of the Working Time Directive stipulates that 'The provisions of [the Framework Health and Safety] Directive 89/391/EEC are fully applicable to the matters referred to in paragraph 2, without prejudice to more stringent and/or specific provisions contained in this Directive'. The matters referred to in para. 2 are '(a) minimum periods of daily rest, weekly rest and annual leave, breaks and maximum weekly working time; and (b) certain aspects of night work, shift work and patterns of work'. The preamble to the Young Workers Directive also makes reference to the Framework Directive.

It would appear that in interpreting the Directives, the ECJ will have regard to the provisions of the Framework Directive and the 'daughter Directives' made pursuant to it. This will give the ECJ the judicial freedom to adopt a contextual approach to the interpretation of the provisions of the Directives, which may result in a meaning being prescribed which could not have been foreseen.

Article 6(1) of the Framework Directive imposes a general obligation on employers to:

take the measures necessary for the safety and health protection of workers, including *prevention* of occupational risks and provision of information and training. . . .
The employer shall be alert to the need to adjust these measures to take account of changing circumstances and aim to improve existing situations (emphasis added).

The emphasis is on *prevention*; assessing risks to the health and safety of workers and avoiding those risks. Article 6(2) of the Framework Directive sets out nine principles of prevention:

(a) avoiding risks,
(b) evaluating risks which cannot be avoided,
(c) combating risks at source,
(d) adapting work to the individual,
(e) adapting to technical progress,
(f) replacing the dangerous by the non-dangerous or less dangerous (substitutability),
(g) developing of a coherent safety policy,
(h) giving collective measures priority over individual measures,
(i) giving appropriate instructions to employees.

The Framework Directive imposes an obligation on employers to undertake a risk assessment to prevent harm to the worker's health and safety. The Framework Directive's requirements on risk assessment were transposed into UK law by the Management of Health and Safety at Work Regulations 1992 (SI 1992/2051). Regulation 3 imposes an obligation on employers to undertake a risk assessment in respect of the health and safety of their employees. In *UK* v *Council of the European Union* (case C-84/94) [1997] IRLR 30 (see chapter 1) the ECJ held that 'health and safety of workers', within the context of art. 118a EC Treaty [art. 137] and the Working Time Directive was to be given a broad scope. This was supported by reference to the Constitution of the World Health Organisation (to which all the Member States belong), in which health is defined as 'a state of complete physical, mental and social well-being which does not consist only in the absence of illness or infirmity'.

The implication of the above is that in interpreting the Working Time Directive (and as a corollary the Young Workers Directive) the ECJ will recognise the ongoing duty of the employer to assess risks in order to prevent harm to the health and safety of workers. The Young Workers Directive explicitly imposes general and specific health and safety obligations on the employers of, *inter alia*, young workers (arts 6 and 7). Since the Working Time Regulations 1998 have been enacted in order to implement the Directives, UK courts will comply with their obligation under *Marleasing SA* v *La Comercial Internacional de Alimentación SA* (case C-106/89) [1990] ECR I-4135 to interpret the Regulations consistently with the Directives, even if this requires distorting the meaning of the Regulations (see chapter 2).

DAILY REST

Adult workers

The entitlement under art. 3 of the Working Time Directive for all adult workers to 11 consecutive hours rest per 24-hour period has been transposed by reg. 10(1) of the Working Time Regulations 1998, which additionally provides that this entitlement is in respect of each 24-hour period 'during which he [the worker] works for his employer'. This simply provides that the entitlement will only arise during a 24-hour period in which a worker is engaged in 'working time' (see chapter 4).

The reference is to each '24-hour period' rather than each 'day' and it follows that the 11 consecutive hours do not have to be during the same calendar day. Therefore, for example, a worker who works 9.00 a.m. to 6.00 p.m. five days each week will have the entitlement measured during the 24-hour period 9.00 a.m. on the first day of the week to 9.00 a.m. the following day, and so on. In this instance, the daily rest period will take place from 6.00 p.m. on the first day to 9.00 a.m. the following day (i.e., 15 hours) and therefore the 11-hour entitlement is satisfied.

Young workers

Article 10(3) of the Young Workers Directive is more generous than art. 3 of the Working Time Directive. It provides that adolescent (young) workers are entitled to 12 consecutive hours' rest during each 24-hour period. This has been transposed by reg. 10(2) of the Working Time Regulations 1998. Regulation 10(3) takes advantage of art. 10(3), which provides that this rest break can be 'interrupted' in the case of 'activities involving periods of work that are split up over the day or are of short duration'.

The government believes that it should not be difficult to establish whether periods of work can reasonably be described as being 'split up over the day' (Consultation Document URN 98/645, para. 98). This will apply to a young shift worker, for example, working 9.00 a.m. to 11.00 a.m. and 8.00 p.m. to 10.00 p.m. over a five-day week; there are nine hours' rest between 11.00 a.m. and 8.00 p.m.

and 11 hours' rest between 10.00 p.m. and the following 9.00 a.m. The concept of 'short duration', which is taken directly from the Directive, could be more problematic and the government states that this 'introduces consideration of relativity which might produce different conclusions if one working arrangement was compared to another. The Regulations therefore leave this expression undefined' (Consultation Document, para. 99).

Derogations

The Working Time and Young Workers Directives enable Member States to disapply the entitlement to a daily rest period or to operate it differently in respect of particular workers in certain circumstances. In transposing the Directives the UK has taken advantage of the vast majority of the available derogations. In the government's view this is because there is 'no reason to deny either business or workers the opportunity of taking up derogations which the Directives allow so as to preserve flexibilities and freedom to organise working time as they wish' (Consultation Document, p. 43). In any event: 'employers have a general duty under health and safety law to protect, so far as is reasonably practicable, the health, safety and welfare at work of their workers' (Consultation Document, para. 138). The ongoing obligation of an employer to assess risks to a worker's health and safety, in the context of the Framework Health and Safety Directive, has been considered above; this obligation will be especially relevant where a derogation disapplies or modifies the entitlement to a daily rest period.

Unmeasured working time Regulation 20 replicates art. 17(1) of the Working Time Directive and provides that reg. 10(1) will not apply to an adult worker where 'on account of the specific characteristics of the activity in which he is engaged, the duration of his working time is not measured or predetermined or can be determined by the worker himself'. The scope of this is discussed in Chapter 3.

Other special cases Regulation 21 takes advantage of art. 17(2)(2.1) and (2)(2.2) of the Working Time Directive and replicates the provisions almost word for word, thus providing that the daily rest entitlement will not apply to certain adult workers, provided the worker concerned is, wherever possible, allowed to take an 'equivalent period of compensatory rest' or, in an exceptional case where this is not possible for 'objective reasons', the worker concerned is afforded 'such protection as may be appropriate in order to safeguard the worker's health and safety' (reg. 24).

An 'equivalent period of compensatory rest' means exactly what it says. An adult worker having 10 hours' continuous rest during one 24-hour period will be entitled to have the one-hour deficiency made good at a later stage. There could be problems associated with a worker whose working week consists of, for example, three 15-hour periods over three consecutive days. Since there is no possibility of the deficiency being made good during the three 24-hour periods that the worker works for the employer, if the worker seeks to enforce the entitlement, a tribunal could make a declaration upholding the worker's complaint. As noted above, there is also an ongoing obligation on the employer to assess risks to a worker's health and safety.

The Regulatory Guidance states that compensatory rest should be provided 'within a reasonable time from when the entitlement was modified — this should usually be possible within a couple of weeks for daily rest' (para. 5.2.5). But reg. 24 does not explicitly provide for compensatory rest to be provided within a *reasonable* period of time, although this could probably be implied.

The government believes that:

in practice 'exceptional circumstances' will be rare, but will also be self-evident. They might arise if a worker left the employment before 'compensatory rest' had been or could be provided, or a business closed down altogether before the rest could be given. Therefore, the presumption must be that a worker concerned is to get an 'equivalent period of compensatory rest' (Consultation Document, para. 147).

The Regulatory Guidance states that this provision could not be used on a 'routine basis' (para. 5.2.5).

The categories of workers covered by reg. 21 are discussed in chapter 3.

Shift workers   A 'shift worker' is defined as 'any worker whose work schedule is part of shift work' (reg. 22(2); art. 2(6)); 'shift work' is defined as 'any method of organising work in shifts whereby workers succeed each other at the same workstations according to a certain pattern, including a rotating pattern, and which may be continuous or discontinuous, entailing the need for workers to work at different times over a given period of days or weeks' (reg. 22(2); art. 2(5)).

Regulation 22 takes advantage of art. 17(2)(2.3) and provides that the daily rest period entitlement for an adult worker under reg. 10(1) will not apply to:

(a)   a shift worker who changes shift and cannot take the rest period between the end of one shift and the start of the next one, or

(b)   a worker engaged in activities involving periods of work split over the day, as may be the case for cleaning staff.

However, in line with reg. 21 there is a requirement that the worker concerned is, wherever possible, allowed to take an 'equivalent period of compensatory rest' which the Regulatory Guidance states should be provided 'within a reasonable time from when the entitlement was modified — this should usually be possible within a couple of weeks' (para. 5.2.5) or, in an exceptional case where this is not possible for 'objective reasons', the worker concerned is afforded 'such protection as may be appropriate in order to safeguard the worker's health and safety' (reg. 24).

This derogation resolves the problematic situation associated with shift workers. For example, an adult worker who works 10.00 a.m. to 2.00 p.m. and 8.00 p.m. to 12 midnight each day will only have a maximum of 10 consecutive hours' rest during a 24-hour period (i.e., 12 midnight to 10.00 a.m. the following day). Regulation 22 derogates from the worker's entitlement to 11 consecutive hours' rest, provided the shift worker concerned is, wherever possible, allowed to take an 'equivalent period of compensatory rest' or that, in an exceptional case where this is not possible for 'objective reasons', the worker concerned is afforded 'such protection as may be appropriate in order to safeguard the worker's health and safety'. Compensatory rest will therefore, in this example, be afforded through the provision of the additional rest break of six hours between 2.00 p.m. and 8.00 p.m.

Collective and workforce agreements   Regulation 23 enables a collective agreement or workforce agreement to modify or exclude an adult worker's entitlement to a daily rest period under reg. 10(1) provided, once again, that the worker concerned is either allowed to take an 'equivalent period of compensatory rest' or, in an exceptional case where this is not possible for 'objective reasons', the worker concerned is afforded 'such protection as may be appropriate in order to safeguard the worker's health and safety' (reg. 24).

Young workers   None of the above derogations apply to a young worker's entitlement under reg. 10(2). Article 13 of the Young Workers Directive enables a Member State to authorise a derogation from the daily rest period for adolescent workers in the event of *force majeure*. This has been transposed by reg. 27 which provides that the entitlement to a daily rest period will not apply to a young worker:

> where his employer requires him to undertake work which no adult worker is available to perform and which—
>
> (a)   is occasioned by either—
>   (i)   an occurrence due to unusual and unforeseeable circumstances, beyond the employer's control; or
>   (ii)   exceptional events, the consequences of which could not have been avoided despite the exercise of all due care by the employer;
> (b)   is of a temporary nature; and
> (c)   must be performed immediately.

Regulation 27(2) provides that in these circumstances the young worker's employer must allow an equivalent period of compensatory rest to be taken within the following three weeks.

All the relevant conditions allowing this derogation to apply have to be satisfied before an employer can rely upon it. It is the government's view that:

> it is not a derogation that could possibly be used to deal with anything other than unique ('one-off') crises that allow for no other reasonable response . . . the derogation is only to be used where there really is no alternative means or method of dealing with a quite unexpected and unpredictable problem. Responding to the aftermath of a terrorist act, or to the effects of a completely unexpected outbreak of illness among a workforce might be relevant circumstances (Consultation Document, para. 153).

This is confirmed by the Regulatory Guidance: 'All the relevant conditions have to apply. Clearly they would only apply in a situation that allowed for no other reasonable response' (para. 5.3.3).

Article 10(4) of the Young Workers Directive also allows a derogation from the daily rest period in respect of young workers provided there are 'objective grounds for so doing and provided that [any young worker concerned is] granted appropriate compensatory rest time'. This derogation only applies to certain specified cases, which includes 'work performed in the context of the armed forces or the police'. The Ministry of Defence expressed concerns to the government that the combat effectiveness of the armed forces would be compromised if young workers serving in the forces were provided with the entitlement to a daily rest period. The government accepted that in this particular case, the necessary 'objective grounds' were present. Regulation 25(2) accordingly provides that the entitlement to a daily rest period does not apply to a young worker serving as a member of the armed forces (i.e., any of the naval, military and air forces of the Crown: reg. 2(1)). However, where the worker is required to work during a period which would otherwise be a rest period, an 'appropriate period of compensatory rest' will be allowed (reg. 25(3)).

Enforcement

An *entitlement* to a daily rest period is created by reg. 10(1) and (2). This differs from other provisions which, rather than create entitlements for workers, impose limits or impose obligations on an employer. For example, reg. 4(1) provides that a worker's working time *shall not* exceed an average of 48 hours for each seven days. Given that the daily rest period is classified as an entitlement, although an employer cannot lawfully require the worker to work during this period (except in accordance with the available derogations), it will not be unlawful for a worker to choose to work during a rest period entitlement. The method of enforcement for an entitlement to a daily rest period is through a worker's complaint to an employment tribunal.

A complaint may be made under reg. 30(1) if the employer has refused to allow a worker to exercise the right to a daily rest period under reg. 10(1) or (2). If the tribunal finds the complaint to be well-founded, it will make a declaration to that effect and has the power to make an award of compensation to the worker (reg. 30(3)). Regulation 30(4) provides that the amount of compensation shall be such as the tribunal considers:

just and equitable in all the circumstances having regard to—
  (a) the employer's default in refusing to permit the worker to exercise his right [e.g., to the daily rest period]; and
  (b) any loss sustained by the worker which is attributable to the matters complained of [e.g., the entitlement to a daily rest period].

There is no limit to the amount of compensation that can be awarded.

The complaint must be made within three months of the date of the act, or failure to act, complained of, although this period may be extended if the tribunal agrees that it was not reasonably practicable to bring the complaint within three months (reg. 30(2)). Special provisions apply to workers serving in the armed forces (reg. 38(2)) for whom the time limit is extended to six months. As well as this direct claim to enforce the entitlement, the worker can also submit a claim to an employment tribunal if he or she is subjected to a detriment, dismissed or selected for redundancy for, *inter alia*, refusing to forgo a right conferred by the

Regulations, bringing proceedings to enforce such a right or alleging that the employer has infringed it. This is by virtue of new ss. 45A, 101A and 105(4A) of the Employment Rights Act 1996, inserted by regs. 31 and 32, discussed in Chapter 5 above.

Regulation 35 provides that any provision in an agreement which purports to exclude or limit the operation of any provision of the Regulations, or preclude a person from making a complaint to a tribunal, is void unless an ACAS conciliation officer has taken action under the Employment Tribunals Act 1996, s. 18, or the parties have signed a compromise agreement which complies with the requirements set out in reg. 35(3).

WEEKLY REST PERIODS

Adult workers

Article 5 of the Working Time Directive requires Member States to take the measures necessary to ensure that 'per each seven-day period, every [adult] worker is entitled to a minimum uninterrupted rest period of 24 hours, plus the 11 hours' daily rest referred to in Article 3'. This equates to a minimum uninterrupted weekly rest period of 35 hours. However, if 'objective, technical or work organisation conditions so justify', a minimum rest period of 24 hours may be applied. This has been transposed by reg. 11 which entitles an adult worker to an 'uninterrupted rest period of not less than 24 hours in each seven-day period during which he works for his employer'. Regulation 11(7) provides that the 24-hour weekly rest period for adult workers is additional to the 11-hour daily rest period 'except where this is justified by objective or technical reasons or reasons concerning the organisation of work'. This is not further defined in the Directive or the Regulations. The Regulatory Guidance states that objective or technical reasons, or reasons concerning the organisation of work 'would have to be inherent in the nature of the work or its desired purpose, rather than created merely to avoid the effect of the Regulations' (para. 5.2.6). In the draft regulations this exception was worded in identical language to that of the Directive: 'except where this is justified by objective, technical or work organisation conditions'; the effect is arguably the same. With regard to the exception contained in the draft regulations the government stated that 'in any case of dispute about whether such a condition applied it would be for the courts to decide'. However, 'the government believes that "work organisation conditions" would always be relevant to any situation where this modification of the entitlement was in fact in order' (Consultation Document, para. 106).

Regulation 11(2) takes advantage of the extended reference period of 14 days for the calculation of the entitlement as provided for in art. 16(1). If the employer decides to take advantage of this extended reference period then the entitlement to a weekly rest period is either:

(a) two uninterrupted rest periods each of not less than 24 hours in each 14-day period during which the worker works for the employer; or
(b) one uninterrupted rest period of not less than 48 hours in each such 14-day period.

Regulation 11(4) sets out when the seven-day period will begin: it will start at the beginning of each week (i.e., at midnight between Sunday and Monday (reg. 11(6)), or as provided in a 'relevant agreement' (i.e., a collective agreement, workforce agreement or any other agreement in writing which is legally enforceable as between the worker and his employer: reg. 2(1) — see chapter 4).

In the case of an adult worker, if the employer determines to take advantage of the extended 14-day reference period, then the 14-day period will begin at midnight between Sunday and Monday every other week (reg. 11(4) and (6)). Regulation 11(5) provides that the first 14-day period will begin on Monday 5 October 1998 if the worker was employed on or before the date on which the Regulations came into force (i.e., 1 October 1998) otherwise it will begin at midnight between the Sunday and Monday in which the worker's employment started.

Young workers

Regulation 11(3) replicates art.10(2) of the Young Workers Directive and provides that a young worker is entitled to 'a rest period of not less than 48 hours, in each seven-day period during which he works for his employer'. It is not possible to extend this seven-day period. The draft regulations provided that the 48-hour minimum rest period 'shall be consecutive if possible', but this does not appear in the final version of the Regulations despite its inclusion in art. 10(2) of the Directive. Regulation 10(4) governs when the seven-day period will start (see above).

With regard to young workers, reg. 11(8) provides that the 48-hour rest period may be interrupted in the case of activities involving periods of work that are split up over the day or are of short duration (this also applies to daily rest periods, see above), and may be reduced where this is justified by technical or organisation reasons (not further defined in the Directive or the Regulations), but not to less than 36 consecutive hours. This transposes art. 10(3) and (2) of the Young Workers Directive respectively. The Regulatory Guidance states that technical or organisation reasons which justify a reduction in the 48-hour rest period to not less than 36 hours must be 'inherent in the nature of the work or its desired purpose, rather than created merely to avoid the effect of the Regulations' (para. 5.3.2).

Article 10(2) of the Young Workers Directive provides that 'The minimum rest period . . . shall in principle include Sunday'. This was also included within art. 5 of the Working Time Directive in respect of adult workers, but it was annulled by the ECJ in *UK* v *Council of the European Union* (case C-84/94) [1996] ECR I-5755 (see chapter 1) because the ECJ did not accept that a Sunday rest day was more closely connected to a worker's health and safety than any other day of the week. Article 10(2) of the Young Workers Directive has not been challenged, but it would probably face a similar destiny. The preamble to the Directive confirms the absence of a link with health and safety:

Whereas, with respect to the weekly rest period, due account should be taken of the diversity of cultural, ethnic, religious and other factors prevailing in the Member States; whereas in particular, it is ultimately for each Member State to decide whether Sunday should be included in the weekly rest period, and if so to what extent.

For this reason, the Regulations do not require young workers' rest days to include Sunday.

Derogations

The same derogations as apply to an adult worker's entitlement to a daily rest period (discussed above) apply to an adult worker's entitlement to a weekly rest period. Where 'compensatory rest' has to be provided under reg. 24, the Regulatory Guidance states that it should be provided 'within a reasonable time from when the entitlement was modified — this should usually be possible within . . . a couple of months for weekly rest' (para. 5.2.5).

In the case of young workers, the only derogation is that which applies in respect of young workers serving in the armed forces: the *force majeure* derogation does not apply.

Enforcement

As with daily rest periods, workers are *entitled* to weekly rest periods in the situations set out in the Regulations. The appropriate method of enforcement of an entitlement is through a worker's complaint to an employment tribunal. All of the enforcement provisions which apply to the enforcement of the entitlement to a daily rest period (see above) will apply to the enforcement of the entitlement to a weekly rest period.

REST BREAKS

Adult workers

Article 4 of the Working Time Directive requires Member States to 'take the measures necessary to ensure that, where the working day is longer than six hours, every [adult] worker is entitled to a rest break, the details of which, including duration and the terms on which it is granted, shall be laid down in collective agreements or agreements between the two sides of industry or, failing that, by national legislation'.

Regulation 12 transposes art. 4 by providing that 'Where an adult worker's daily working time is more than six hours, he is entitled to a rest break' (reg. 12(1)). The concept of 'working time' is discussed in chapter 4. There may be a conflict between reg. 12(1) and art. 4, in that reg. 12(1) refers to 'working time' whereas art. 4 refers to 'working day'.

Regulation 12(2) provides that the details of the rest break, including its duration and the terms on which it is granted, shall be laid down in a collective agreement or a workforce agreement. This complies with art. 4 which stipulates this as the method of implementation. However, art. 4 continues 'or, failing that, by national legislation'. Regulation 12(3) therefore provides that where there is no collective agreement or workforce agreement under reg. 12(2) then the rest break will be 'an uninterrupted period of not less than 20 minutes, and the worker is entitled to spend it away from his workstation if he has one'.

This 20-minute period may be satisfactory for a worker employed for around six hours, but what would the position be of a worker employed for well in excess of six hours? Would one 20-minute rest break be sufficient, bearing in mind the employer's ongoing health and safety obligation under the Framework Health and Safety Directive? In Germany, employees working between six and nine hours per day must be granted a break of at least 30 minutes' duration in total, increasing to 45 minutes for those working more than nine hours. Break times may be divided up into periods of not less than 15 minutes. In the Netherlands there is an entitlement to 30 consecutive minutes where the working day is at least 5.5 hours, increasing to 45 minutes where it is over eight hours, and 60 minutes where it exceeds 10 hours (in both cases at least 30 minutes must be consecutive). In Ireland there is an entitlement to a break of at least 15 minutes where employees work for more than 4.5 hours, and at least 30 minutes for those working more than 6 hours. The UK's implementation of this entitlement may therefore be inadequate.

Pattern of work

Article 13 of the Working Time Directive provides that:

> Member States shall take the measures necessary to ensure that an employer who intends to organise work according to a certain pattern takes account of the general principle of adapting work to the worker, with a view, in particular, to alleviating monotonous work and work at a predetermined work-rate, depending on the type of activity, and of safety and health requirements, *especially as regards breaks during working time* (emphasis added).

Although art. 13 appears in the section of the Directive which deals with night and shift work, it is likely to have general application, in view of the fact that the specific examples, 'monotonous work and work at predetermined work-rate', are not exclusively confined to night workers and shift workers.

Bercusson has referred to this general principle of adapting work to the workers as the 'humanisation of work', requiring employers to ensure that workers engaged in, for example, monotonous work and work at a predetermined work-rate are part of the equation when the employer considers how that work is organised. Article 13 specifically provides that for this type of work employers must take into account the health and safety requirements of their workers, especially with regard to breaks during working time.

This has been transposed by reg. 8 which requires that an employer ensures that workers who are engaged in work which is organised according to a pattern which is such as to put the workers' health and safety at risk, in particular because the work is monotonous or the work-rate is predetermined, are given adequate rest breaks.

There is no elaboration in the Regulations of what constitutes 'adequate rest breaks' but the government states that this may mean employers should consider providing such workers with more short breaks as opposed to a longer continuous break (Consultation Document, para. 117). The Regulatory Guidance states that 'where the pattern of work involves uninterruptible or monotonous activities (for example a single task on a continuous production line), which puts the health and safety of a worker at risk, an employer needs to consider granting regular breaks in order to reduce those risks' (para. 6.1.3).

It is worth noting that the particular dangers of monotonous work have been recognised at common law in relation to an employer's general duty of care to employees for many years. In *Caswell* v *Powell Duffryn Associated Collieries* [1940] AC 152 Lord Wright, discussing contributory negligence said:

> What is all-important is to adapt the standard of what is negligence to the facts, and to give due regard to the actual conditions under which men work in a factory or mine, to the long hours and the fatigue, to the slackening of attention which naturally comes from constant repetition of the same operation, to the noise and confusion in which the man works, to his own pre-occupation in what he is actually doing at the cost perhaps of some inattention to his own safety. (pp. 178–9)

Young workers

Regulation 12(4) transposes art. 12 of the Young Workers Directive and provides that where a young worker's daily working time is more than four and a half hours, there is an entitlement to a rest break of at least 30 minutes, which shall be consecutive if possible, to be spent away from the workstation if the worker has one. Unlike the Working Time Directive, the actual duration of the break is specifically set out in the Young Workers Directive. Article 8(4) of the Young Workers Directive provides that 'where a young person is employed by more than one employer, working days and working time shall be cumulative'. Regulation 12(5) takes this into account when calculating a young worker's total working time for the purposes of attaining the right to a rest break: 'If, on any day, a young worker is employed by more than one employer, his daily working time shall be determined for the purpose of paragraph (4) by aggregating the number of hours worked by him for each employer'. The government believes that this puts an employer under an effective duty to make reasonable enquiries of any young worker to ensure that an entitlement to a rest break is being observed, taking into account the worker's total working time for any relevant employer concerned (Consultation Document, para. 116). The Regulatory Guidance states that 'It would be reasonable for an employer to make enquiries of any adolescent worker to ascertain whether an entitlement to a rest break is being observed, taking account of an adolescent's total working time' (para. 6.3.1). However, it should be stressed that reg. 12(4) gives rise to an *entitlement* rather than a limitation or mandatory obligation on the employer and therefore the employer's duty will only arise where the worker takes advantage of, or seeks to take advantage of, the entitlement.

Derogations

For adult workers, all the derogations discussed above in respect of entitlement to a daily rest period apply to rest breaks, with the exception of the derogation in reg. 22 relating to shift workers. Where the entitlement to a rest break is excluded under reg. 21 the worker must, wherever possible, be allowed to take an 'equivalent period of compensatory rest' (reg. 24), which, according to the Regulatory Guidance, should be provided 'within a reasonable time from when the entitlement was modified — this should usually be possible within a couple of

weeks' (para. 6.2.4). If, in an exceptional case compensatory rest is not possible
for 'objective reasons', the worker concerned must be afforded 'such protection as
may be appropriate in order to safeguard the worker's health and safety' (reg. 24).
Collective agreements and workforce agreements can, by reg. 23, derogate from
the entitlement to rest breaks, but subject to reg. 24 (compensatory rest).

For young workers, the *force majeure* derogation set out in reg. 27 applies to
rest breaks, but the derogation in respect of young workers serving in the armed
forces (reg. 25) does not apply.

Enforcement

As with daily rest periods, workers are *entitled* to rest breaks in the situations set
out in the Regulations. The appropriate method of enforcement of an entitlement
is through a worker's complaint to an employment tribunal. All of the enforcement
provisions which apply to the entitlement to a daily rest period will apply to
enforcement of the entitlement to a rest break.

Chapter Seven
Annual Leave

It would probably surprise most workers to learn that until the Working Time Regulations 1998 came into force they had no statutory right to any holiday at all, not even bank holidays, much less any paid holiday. This was not always the case. From the Trade Boards Act 1909 onwards there was a system of regulation of terms and conditions in the 'sweated trades', which were areas of employment characterised by low pay, poor terms and conditions, no system of collective bargaining and, frequently, the fact that the majority of the workers were women. While the trade boards' main focus was on pay, in 1918 they were given powers to fix other terms and conditions, including holidays, and the number of boards and industries covered was greatly expanded. In 1945 this system was replaced by wages councils under the Wages Councils Act 1945. Agricultural workers were covered by a separate Agricultural Wages Board, which operated on the same lines. In their heyday, wages councils covered over 20 per cent of the workforce and regulated wage rates, overtime rates, paid holiday entitlements and other terms and conditions. The standard of four weeks' paid holiday, which was widely adopted in contracts of employment, probably had its origins in the standards laid down by wages councils. The Wages Act 1986 removed wages councils' powers to set any terms and conditions except for a basic rate of pay and in 1993 they were abolished altogether, except for the Agricultural Wages Board.

It is fairly clear that since 1986 a lot of workers who were previously covered by wages councils have seen their entitlements to paid holidays reduced. Part-time workers have always been worse off than full-time workers in this regard. The government's Consultation Document estimated that 0.7 million full-time and 1.8 million part-time workers were entitled to less than three weeks' paid leave per annum, and that 1.1 million full-time and 2.0 million part-time workers had less than four weeks' paid leave (URN 98/645, annex E2, para. 2.13). There are therefore a lot of workers who will benefit from the Working Time Directive's requirement to give workers three weeks' paid leave, rising to four weeks in November 1999. The cost to employers of implementing the new entitlements to annual leave is reckoned to be £0.47 billion, rising to £0.87 billion in 1999, when the entitlement is raised from three to four weeks.

Article 7 of the Working Time Directive simply states that workers have a right to paid annual leave and that this cannot be 'bought out' by giving the worker pay in lieu except where the contract terminates. Such a simple concept nonetheless gives rise to many technical questions in its implementation: When does the entitlement arise? How long does it last? What control does an employer have over when leave is taken? How is the leave year measured? These issues are dealt with in regs 13–17 of the Working Time Regulations 1998.

THREE WEEKS OR FOUR WEEKS?

Article 7 of the Working Time Directive fixes the paid holiday entitlement at four weeks. However, a temporary derogation was permitted under art. 18(1)(b)(ii) for the first three years in which the Directive was in operation — i.e., from 23 November 1996 to 23 November 1999. The government decided to take advantage of this concession, but was so late in implementing the Directive that only a little over a year remains for it to be used (reg. 13(2)). Member States cannot take advantage of any derogations in a Directive until they have actually taken steps to implement it, and so it follows that for the period 23 November 1996 to 1 October 1998, the entitlement should have been four weeks. It seems likely that art. 7 of the Working Time Directive is sufficiently precise and unconditional for the principle of direct effect to apply, in which case the government must be at risk of claims by any workers employed by an emanation of the State who have not received four weeks' paid leave (see *Shevlane* v *Mid-Kent College of Higher and Further Education* (6 March 1998 EAT 242/98 unreported) discussed in chapter 2). Workers in the private sector who were denied their entitlement might be able to claim compensation from the government for denial of their rights (see chapter 2).

The transitional period

What happens on 23 November 1999 when the entitlement goes up to four weeks? Regulation 13(2)(b) provides that in those circumstances the worker is entitled to such proportion of a fourth week as is equivalent to the proportion of the year starting on 23 November 1998 which has elapsed at the start of the leave year beginning after that date. This is probably explicable only by an example. One is given in the Regulatory Guidance (para. 7.1):

> If a worker's leave year starts on 1 January and they work five days a week, then their entitlement for 1999 is three weeks (15 days) + a portion of a further week.
>   The additional part of the week is calculated by multiplying the number of working days in the worker's normal working week by the number of days between 23 November and the start of the leave year, divided by the number of days in a year.
>   In this case, there are 39 days between 23 November and the start of the leave year, so the calculation is:

$$5 \text{ days} \times 39/365 = 0.53$$

This is rounded up to the nearest day, i.e. 1 day. This means that the worker is entitled to 16 days' paid annual leave for the leave year 1999.

Provision for rounding up is made in reg. 13(6): the entitlement is always rounded *up* to the nearest whole day even if the fraction is less than one half.

Part-time workers and workers with varying hours

There is no definition in the Regulations of what is meant by a week's leave. The Regulatory Guidance says that it 'should be equivalent to the time a worker would work in a week . . . where a worker works irregular hours, the worker would have a right to annual leave that would allow them to be away from their place of work for a week' (para. 7.1.4). It is surprising that no definition is given of this key concept when the related concept of a week's pay is defined (by reference to the Employment Rights Act 1996, see below). It may be uncontroversial to suggest that a part-timer working two days a week should be entitled to six days' paid holiday, as this is equivalent to allowing the worker to be away for three weeks, but real problems could arise with workers who have varying hours of work. It would be prudent to reach some agreement on what would constitute a week's leave for such a worker. Although it would in theory be open to a tribunal or court to find otherwise, it is likely that such an agreement would influence any decision if it were challenged.

There is, of course, no minimum hours requirement for entitlements under the Working Time Regulations 1998, so part-time workers who only do a few hours a week are nonetheless entitled to their paid holiday. While domestic servants are excluded from many of the provisions of the Regulations, they are entitled to paid leave (reg. 19). This is likely to be overlooked by many people who rely on the visit of a weekly cleaner to their homes and who are used only to paying when work is performed!

THE LEAVE YEAR

It is open to employers and workers to agree the date of the leave year by means of a relevant agreement — which could, of course, include a written contract of employment (reg. 13(3)). In default of any such agreement, reg. 13(3) provides that the leave year will run from 1 October every year for workers already employed by 1 October 1998, and from the date on which employment commenced for anyone employed after 1 October 1998. There is an exception for agricultural workers, whose leave year is either fixed by an agricultural wages order or else runs from a default date of 6 April each year, unless a relevant agreement makes other arrangements (art. 13(4); sch. 2).

Where there is a relevant agreement, again a transitional provision is needed to deal with workers who are taken on after the beginning of a leave year. This is dealt with by a parallel provision to the regulation dealing with the change from three to four weeks. Article 13(5) provides that in these circumstances, the worker is entitled to such proportion of the three-week or four-week period as is equal to the proportion of the leave year remaining. For example, suppose that the leave year runs from 1 October 1998 and the worker is taken on to work a regular five days a week on 1 March 1999. The usual entitlement in the leave year would be three weeks, as the leave year will end on 30 September 1999, before the four-week entitlement comes into play. There are 214 days between 1 March and the start of the next leave year, so the calculation is:

$$15 \text{ days} \times 214/365 = 8.8$$

Rounding this up to the nearest day means that the worker will be entitled to nine days' paid leave up to the end of the leave year.

Termination during the leave year

If a worker's contract is terminated during a leave year, it will be necessary to establish whether the worker has taken more or less than his or her entitlement at that date. The consequences are dealt with in reg. 14. The worker's entitlement is calculated by looking at what proportion of the leave year has expired to decide what proportion of the paid leave period the worker was entitled to. The amount of leave actually taken by the worker in the leave year is then subtracted. The formula is laid out in art. 14(3)(b) as follows:

$$(A \times B) - C$$

where:
A is the period of leave to which the worker is entitled in the leave year;
B is the proportion of the leave year which has expired on the date of termination;
C is the period of leave already taken by the worker.

To adapt the example used above, suppose that the leave year runs from 1 October 1998, that the worker works a regular five days a week, and this time, that the contract is terminated on 1 March 1999. The usual entitlement in the leave year would be three weeks, as the leave year would end on 30 September 1999, before the four-week entitlement came into play, so $A = 15$.

Let us suppose that the worker has taken one week's leave (five days) already during the year, so $C = 5$. The expired portion of the leave year (1 October 1998 to 1 March 1999) is 152 days, so $B = 152/365$, which is 0.42.

$$(A \times B) - C = (15 \times 0.42) - 5 = 1.3$$

In these circumstances, art. 14(2) states that the employer must make a payment in lieu to the worker to make up for the lost entitlement. This is the only situation where payment can be made in lieu of holiday entitlement. The payment to be made can either be such sum as is provided for in a relevant agreement, or a sum calculated in accordance with reg. 16, which cross-refers to ss. 221–4 of the Employment Rights Act 1996 on the calculation of a week's pay (suitably altered to take account of the fact that the Regulations apply to 'workers', not just 'employees'). The general effect of these sections can be summarised as follows:

(a)   If a worker has normal working hours and the same pay whatever the amount of work done, a week's pay is the amount payable for the normal working hours in a week.

(b)   If a worker has normal working hours, but the rate of pay varies according to the amount of work done (e.g., piece workers), a week's pay is the average of the pay received for normal working hours in the 12 weeks preceding the first day of the leave period.

(c) If a worker has normal working hours, but the rate of pay varies according to the time of day when the work is done (e.g., shift workers), a week's pay is the average of the pay received for normal working hours in the 12 weeks preceding the first day of the leave period.

(d) If a worker has no normal working hours, a week's pay is the average weekly remuneration for the 12 weeks preceding the first day of the leave period. If the worker did not work during all of those weeks, earlier weeks are counted until there are 12 to average out.

Unlike reg. 13, there is no provision in reg. 14 to state that the entitlement is to be rounded up. It could therefore be argued that there should be no rounding, in that the omission must be intentional. On the other hand, it could be argued that the rounding up should apply by analogy to art. 13. If so, however, this would not always work to the worker's advantage. It would in the example above, because the worker would be entitled to two days' pay instead of 1.3 days' pay. But if the worker has taken *more* leave than that to which he or she was entitled on termination, art. 14(4) provides that a relevant agreement may require the worker to compensate the employer, by payment, or undertaking additional work, or such other means as are specified in the agreement.

To avoid complexity, employers and workers may well feel that the question of compensation for leave entitlement on termination is best dealt with by a relevant agreement. It would be wise in such an agreement to make a decision about what happens to fractions of days. Another possible source of confusion is the reference in reg. 14(1)(b) to 'the date on which termination takes effect' for the purposes of the calculation of leave entitlement. This phrase is not defined in the Regulations, and could well give rise to disputes over whether notice periods are to be counted in or not, if not provided for in a relevant agreement.

As the right to paid leave is an absolute entitlement, the circumstances leading to the termination are irrelevant. Workers dismissed without notice for gross misconduct will nonetheless qualify for compensation if they have not had their statutory leave entitlement at the date of termination. An employer has no right to be compensated by a worker who has taken more than his or her leave at the date of termination if there is no relevant agreement to that effect. This may mean that employers will want to consider controlling how and when workers exercise their entitlement, to be considered next.

QUALIFICATION AND NOTICE

Qualification for leave entitlement

Any worker who is within the scope of the Working Time Regulations 1998 is in principle entitled to paid annual leave. There are no exclusions for those with unmeasured working time such as self-managing executives or family workers. However, the Directive says nothing about whether or not a qualifying period of employment should be set, leaving this to Member States to decide. The Conservative government argued that it would therefore be reasonable to require a worker to have accumulated 49 weeks of continuous service before becoming entitled to three weeks' paid leave in a leave year. Some employers have also argued that a one-year qualification period is necessary to avoid difficulties which would otherwise be faced by industries with a high turnover of staff, such as construction. At the other end of the spectrum, the TUC argued that the entitlement should arise on day 1, in line with their general policy that there should be no qualifying periods for statutory employment protection rights (a policy which was adopted at one time by the Labour Party as well). Temporary workers in particular might never accumulate sufficient service to qualify for paid leave if there was a long qualifying period.

The government has chosen a middle way on this, fixing on 13 weeks of continuous employment as the qualification period (reg. 13(7)). Any week in which the worker's relations with the employer have been governed by a contract will count: there is no requirement that the worker should have worked for the whole week, or even part of it, since the week could be governed by a contract even if the worker was unfit through illness to work. The existence of this continuous service requirement will exclude some casual or on-call workers, if they are unable to demonstrate that their work is performed in the context of an overall 'umbrella' contract (see chapter 3), but temporary workers who obtain employment through an agency will normally be able to treat the agency as employer in these circumstances and will receive an entitlement to paid annual leave from it (reg. 36, see above).

Notice

So far as arrangements for giving notice of leave are concerned, the most important point to note is that reg. 15(5) allows employers and workers to make their own arrangements by means of a relevant agreement. This is clearly the most sensible option, particularly where there are existing contractual arrangements. If not, the default position allows an employer to stipulate when the leave is to be taken, provided that the notice is twice as long as the period of leave which the employer is requiring the worker to take. This allows the employer to stipulate, for example, that the period between Christmas and the New Year and public holidays such as bank holidays are part of the statutory entitlement. Under the draft Regulations, the employer would have had to give at least four weeks' notice, whatever period of leave was to be taken, and the notice would have had to be in writing. Since there is no opportunity for the worker to give a counter-notice, it seems unfortunate that this was watered down. It means, for example, that an employer who can see a temporary downturn in work coming could respond by giving workers two days' notice on Tuesday to take Friday as a holiday to be deducted from their annual entitlement. Indeed, the way that reg. 15 gives complete primacy to the wishes of the employer appears to mean that it would be open to an employer to stipulate all the leave dates for the year, thus ensuring that workers never get in the position of taking more leave than they are entitled to on any particular date, or even to require that leave is taken only after 49 weeks' service! If so, it is somewhat inconsistent with the concept of the worker becoming entitled to paid leave after 13 weeks.

If the employer has not given notice which covers all the worker's entitlement, then reg. 15(1) states that the worker will be entitled to take leave after giving the employer notice which is at least twice as long as the period of leave to be taken.

But in this case, the employer has a right to refuse the leave, provided that a counter-notice is served on the worker as much in advance of the leave period as the length of that period (reg. 15(3) and (4)). The general idea is that if the worker gives two weeks' notice of wishing to take one week's leave, the employer has a week in which to come back and refuse. This is not how it would necessarily work, however. Suppose that on 1 January the worker asks to take 15 June as a holiday because it is a wedding anniversary. The employer can apparently wait until 13 June to give notice that this is not allowed. The fact that none of these notices has to be given in writing exacerbates the position and increases the opportunities for dispute.

Agricultural workers are outside the ambit of reg. 15, being covered instead by sch. 2, which means that the issue will be covered by an agricultural wages order or a relevant agreement.

RELATIONSHIP TO CONTRACTUAL PAID LEAVE

The entitlement to paid annual leave under the Regulations is not additional to any existing rights to contractual paid leave. Thus reg. 16(5) stipulates that any payments which an employer makes under the Regulations will go towards discharging any liability to pay contractual remuneration for the leave period, and vice versa. Since it is possible that contractual paid leave could give a worker an entitlement to more pay than would constitute a week's pay under the Employment Rights Act 1996, ss. 221–4, reg. 16(4) makes it clear that the worker would be able to claim the higher amount. Regulation 17 further provides that the worker can exercise his or her statutory right in combination with any contractual right, taking advantage of whichever is the most favourable in any particular respect. This could be particularly relevant in relation to notice provisions.

ENFORCEMENT

The right to paid annual leave under the Regulations is an entitlement only. In other words, while the worker must be allowed to take it, the employer commits no wrong if the worker chooses not to take it. There is no overriding limit in the Working Time Directive to prevent people from working for more than 49 weeks a year (or 48 from November 1999).

If a worker fails to use the full annual entitlement, there is no statutory right to carry it forward: reg. 13(9)(a) states that leave may only be taken in the leave year in which it is due. This does not stop employers and workers reaching agreement which would allow a carry-forward, but the worker's rights would then depend on the contract, not on the Regulations.

Regulation 13(9)(b) stresses that the leave entitlement may not be replaced by a payment in lieu. This provision (which is required by art.7(2) of the Working Time Directive) was criticised by the Institute of Personnel Development in its response to the Consultation Document, on the grounds that it would prevent an employer from compensating a worker who agreed to take less than his or her entitlement for operational reasons. This shows precisely why that limitation is necessary: otherwise, workers would frequently be under pressure to accept extra pay instead of a holiday and the health and safety policy underpinning the Regulations would be subverted.

That said, there is a real difficulty inherent in the remedies pertaining if the worker is discouraged from exercising his or her right to leave. If the worker is subjected to any detriment or is dismissed on this account, the employer would be liable under ss. 45A or 101A of the Employment Rights Act 1996 (inserted by regs 31 and 32). In the case of detriment, the tribunal has the power to make a declaration and an award of compensation, being such amount as is just and equitable having regard, *inter alia*, to the nature of the infringement: this is by virtue of the Employment Rights Act 1996, s. 49, which also states that the usual rules relating to mitigation of loss apply, suggesting that economic loss is the main criterion. The point is that if the only detriment to the worker is that the paid leave was refused, the obvious way to compensate him or her would seem to be to require leave to be given — but the tribunal has no power to do this. The tribunal's power is limited to a monetary award. There must be a danger that the tribunal may award only a sum equivalent to the worker's pay for the holiday which was refused: but if this were the case, it would in effect allow the employer to buy out the worker's paid leave entitlement. It is to be hoped that in these circumstances a more generous award will be seen as just and equitable.

An employee who is dismissed for exercising rights to paid annual leave will be able to bring an unfair dismissal claim under s. 101A. Such a dismissal will be automatically unfair and there is no qualifying period of service to claim. This option is not open to any worker covered by the Regulations who is not an employee: such a worker would have to bring a claim under s. 45A that the termination of the contract caused a detriment to him or her. In these circumstances, compensation will be subject to the same limit as if it were an unfair dismissal claim.

Appendix One
Text of the Working Time Regulations 1998

Statutory instrument 1998/1833.

Made	*30th July 1998*
Laid before Parliament	*30th July 1998*
Coming into force	*1st October 1998*

ARRANGEMENT OF REGULATIONS

PART I
GENERAL

PART IV
MISCELLANEOUS

PART V
SPECIAL CLASSES OF PERSON

SCHEDULES

The Secretary of State, being a Minister designated for the purposes of section 2(2) of the European Communities Act 1972 in relation to measures relating to the organization of working time and measures relating to the employment of children and young persons, in exercise of the powers conferred on him by that provision hereby makes the following Regulations—

PART I
GENERAL

1. Citation, commencement and extent
    (1) These Regulations may be cited as the Working Time Regulations 1998 and shall come into force on 1st October 1998.
    (2) These Regulations extend to Great Britain only.

2. Interpretation

(1)   In these Regulations—

'the 1996 Act' means the Employment Rights Act 1996;

'adult worker' means a worker who has attained the age of 18;

'the armed forces' means any of the naval, military and air forces of the Crown;

'calendar year' means the period of twelve months beginning with 1st January in any year;

'the civil protection services' includes the police, fire brigades and ambulance services, the security and intelligence services, customs and immigration officers, the prison service, the coastguard, and lifeboat crew and other voluntary rescue services;

'collective agreement' means a collective agreement within the meaning of section 178 of the Trade Union and Labour Relations (Consolidation) Act 1992, the trade union parties to which are independent trade unions within the meaning of section 5 of that Act;

'day' means a period of 24 hours beginning at midnight;

'employer', in relation to a worker, means the person by whom the worker is (or, where the employment has ceased, was) employed;

'employment', in relation to a worker, means employment under his contract, and

'employed' shall be construed accordingly;

'night time', in relation to a worker, means a period—

(a)   the duration of which is not less than seven hours, and

(b)   which includes the period between midnight and 5 a.m.,

which is determined for the purposes of these Regulations by a relevant agreement, or, in default of such a determination, the period between 11 p.m. and 6 a.m.;

'night work' means work during night time;

'night worker' means a worker—

(a)   who, as a normal course, works at least three hours of his daily working time during night time, or

(b)   who is likely, during night time, to work at least such proportion of his annual working time as may be specified for the purposes of these Regulations in a collective agreement or a workforce agreement;

and, for the purpose of paragraph (a) of this definition, a person works hours as a normal course (without prejudice to the generality of that expression) if he works such hours on the majority of days on which he works;

'relevant agreement', in relation to a worker, means a workforce agreement which applies to him, any provision of a collective agreement which forms part of a contract between him and his employer, or any other agreement in writing which is legally enforceable as between the worker and his employer;

'relevant training' means work experience provided pursuant to a training course or programme, training for employment, or both, other than work experience or training—

(a)   the immediate provider of which is an educational institution or a person whose main business is the provision of training, and

(b)   which is provided on a course run by that institution or person;

'rest period', in relation to a worker, means a period which is not working time, other than a rest break or leave to which the worker is entitled under these Regulations;
'worker' means an individual who has entered into or works under (or, where the employment has ceased, worked under)—

(a)   a contract of employment; or

(b)   any other contract, whether express or implied and (if it is express) whether oral or in writing, whereby the individual undertakes to do or perform personally any work or services for another party to the contract whose status is not by virtue of the contract that of a client or customer of any profession or business undertaking carried on by the individual;

and any reference to a worker's contract shall be construed accordingly;
'worker employed in agriculture' has the same meaning as in the Agricultural Wages Act 1948 or the Agricultural Wages (Scotland) Act 1949, and a reference to a worker partly employed in agriculture is to a worker employed in agriculture whose employer also employs him for non-agricultural purposes;
'workforce agreement' means an agreement between an employer and workers employed by him or their representatives in respect of which the conditions set out in Schedule 1 to these Regulations are satisfied;
'working time', in relation to a worker, means—

(a)   any period during which he is working, at his employer's disposal and carrying out his activity or duties,

(b)   any period during which he is receiving relevant training, and

(c)   any additional period which is to be treated as working time for the purpose of these Regulations under a relevant agreement;

and 'work' shall be construed accordingly;
'Working Time Directive' means Council Directive 93/104/EC of 23rd November 1993 concerning certain aspects of the organization of working time;
'young worker' means a worker who has attained the age of 15 but not the age of 18 and who, as respects England and Wales, is over compulsory school age (construed in accordance with section 8 of the Education Act 1996) and, as respects Scotland, is over school age (construed in accordance with section 31 of the Education (Scotland) Act 1980), and
'Young Workers Directive' means Council Directive 94/33/EC of 22nd June 1994 on the protection of young people at work.

(2)   In the absence of a definition in these Regulations, words and expressions used in particular provisions which are also used in corresponding provisions of the Working Time Directive or the Young Workers Directive have the same meaning as they have in those corresponding provisions.

(3)   In these Regulations—

(a)   a reference to a numbered regulation is to the regulation in these Regulations bearing that number;

(b)   a reference in a regulation to a numbered paragraph is to the paragraph in that regulation bearing that number; and

(c)   a reference in a paragraph to a lettered sub-paragraph is to the sub-paragraph in that paragraph bearing that letter.

PART II
RIGHTS AND OBLIGATIONS CONCERNING WORKING TIME

3. General

The provisions of this Part have effect subject to the exceptions provided for in Part III of these Regulations.

4. Maximum weekly working time

(1) Subject to regulation 5, a worker's working time, including overtime, in any reference period which is applicable in his case shall not exceed an average of 48 hours for each seven days.

(2) An employer shall take all reasonable steps, in keeping with the need to protect the health and safety of workers, to ensure that the limit specified in paragraph (1) is complied with in the case of each worker employed by him in relation to whom it applies.

(3) Subject to paragraphs (4) and (5) and any agreement under regulation 23(b), the reference periods which apply in the case of a worker are—

(a) where a relevant agreement provides for the application of this regulation in relation to successive periods of 17 weeks, each such period, or

(b) in any other case, any period of 17 weeks in the course of his employment.

(4) Where a worker has worked for his employer for less than 17 weeks, the reference period applicable in his case is the period that has elapsed since he started work for his employer.

(5) Paragraphs (3) and (4) shall apply to a worker who is excluded from the scope of certain provisions of these Regulations by regulation 21 as if for each reference to 17 weeks there were substituted a reference to 26 weeks.

(6) For the purposes of this regulation, a worker's average working time for each seven days during a reference period shall be determined according to the formula—

$$\frac{A + B}{C}$$

where—

A is the aggregate number of hours comprised in the worker's working time during the course of the reference period;

B is the aggregate number of hours comprised in his working time during the course of the period beginning immediately after the end of the reference period and ending when the number of days in that subsequent period on which he has worked equals the number of excluded days during the reference period; and

C is the number of weeks in the reference period.

(7) In paragraph (6), 'excluded days' means days comprised in—

(a) any period of annual leave taken by the worker in exercise of his entitlement under regulation 13;

(b) any period of sick leave taken by the worker;

(c) any period of maternity leave taken by the worker; and

(d) any period in respect of which the limit specified in paragraph (1) did not apply in relation to the worker by virtue of regulation 5.

5. Agreement to exclude the maximum

(1)   The limit specified in regulation 4(1) shall not apply in relation to a worker who has agreed with his employer in writing that it should not apply in his case, provided that the employer complies with the requirements of paragraph (4).

(2)   An agreement for the purposes of paragraph (1)—

(a)   may either relate to a specified period or apply indefinitely; and

(b)   subject to any provision in the agreement for a different period of notice, shall be terminable by the worker by giving not less than seven days' notice to his employer in writing.

(3)   Where an agreement for the purposes of paragraph (1) makes provision for the termination of the agreement after a period of notice, the notice period provided for shall not exceed three months.

(4)   The requirements referred to in paragraph (1) are that the employer—

(a)   maintains up-to-date records which—

(i)   identify each of the workers whom he employs who has agreed that the limit specified in regulation 4(1) should not apply in his case;

(ii)   set out any terms on which the worker agreed that the limit should not apply; and

(iii)   specify the number of hours worked by him for the employer during each reference period since the agreement came into effect (excluding any period which ended more than two years before the most recent entry in the records);

(b)   permits any inspector appointed by the Health and Safety Executive or any other authority which is responsible under regulation 28 for the enforcement of these Regulations to inspect those records on request; and

(c)   provides any such inspector with such information as he may request regarding any case in which a worker has agreed that the limit specified in regulation 4(1) should not apply in his case.

6. Length of night work

(1)   A night worker's normal hours of work in any reference period which is applicable in his case shall not exceed an average of eight hours for each 24 hours.

(2)   An employer shall take all reasonable steps, in keeping with the need to protect the health and safety of workers, to ensure that the limit specified in paragraph (1) is complied with in the case of each night worker employed by him.

(3)   The reference periods which apply in the case of a night worker are—

(a)   where a relevant agreement provides for the application of this regulation in relation to successive periods of 17 weeks, each such period, or

(b)   in any other case, any period of 17 weeks in the course of his employment.

(4)   Where a worker has worked for his employer for less than 17 weeks, the reference period applicable in his case is the period that has elapsed since he started work for his employer.

(5)   For the purposes of this regulation, a night worker's average normal hours of work for each 24 hours during a reference period shall be determined according to the formula—

$$\frac{A}{B - C}$$

where—

A is the number of hours during the reference period which are normal working hours for that worker;

B is the number of days during the reference period, and

C is the total number of hours during the reference period comprised in rest periods spent by the worker in pursuance of his entitlement under regulation 11, divided by 24.

(6)   A night worker's normal hours of work for the purposes of this regulation are his normal working hours for the purposes of the 1996 Act in a case where section 234 of that Act (which provides for the interpretation of normal working hours in the case of certain employees) applies to him.

(7)   An employer shall ensure that no night worker employed by him whose work involves special hazards or heavy physical or mental strain works for more than eight hours in any 24-hour period during which the night worker performs night work.

(8)   For the purposes of paragraph (7), the work of a night worker shall be regarded as involving special hazards or heavy physical or mental strain if—

(a)   it is identified as such in—

(i)   a collective agreement, or

(ii)   a workforce agreement,

which takes account of the specific effects and hazards of night work, or

(b)   it is recognised in a risk assessment made by the employer under regulation 3 of the Management of Health and Safety at Work Regulations 1992 as involving a significant risk to the health or safety of workers employed by him.

7. Health assessment and transfer of night workers to day work

(1)   An employer—

(a)   shall not assign an adult worker to work which is to be undertaken during periods such that the worker will become a night worker unless—

(i)   the employer has ensured that the worker will have the opportunity of a free health assessment before he takes up the assignment; or

(ii)   the worker had a health assessment before being assigned to work to be undertaken during such periods on an earlier occasion, and the employer has no reason to believe that that assessment is no longer valid, and

(b)   shall ensure that each night worker employed by him has the opportunity of a free health assessment at regular intervals of whatever duration may be appropriate in his case.

(2)   Subject to paragraph (4), an employer—

(a)   shall not assign a young worker to work during the period between 10 p.m. and 6 a.m. ('the restricted period') unless—

(i)   the employer has ensured that the young worker will have the opportunity of a free assessment of his health and capacities before he takes up the assignment; or

(ii)   the young worker had an assessment of his health and capacities before being assigned to work during the restricted period on an earlier occasion, and the employer has no reason to believe that that assessment is no longer valid; and

(b)   shall ensure that each young worker employed by him and assigned to work during the restricted period has the opportunity of a free assessment of his health and capacities at regular intervals of whatever duration may be appropriate in his case.

(3)   For the purposes of paragraphs (1) and (2), an assessment is free if it is at no cost to the worker to whom it relates.

(4)   The requirements in paragraph (2) do not apply in a case where the work a young worker is assigned to do is of an exceptional nature.

(5)   No person shall disclose an assessment made for the purposes of this regulation to any person other than the worker to whom it relates, unless—

(a)   the worker has given his consent in writing to the disclosure, or

(b)   the disclosure is confined to a statement that the assessment shows the worker to be fit—

(i)   in a case where paragraph (1)(a)(i) or (2)(a)(i) applies, to take up an assignment, or

(ii)   in a case where paragraph (1)(b) or (2)(b) applies, to continue to undertake an assignment.

(6)   Where—

(a)   a registered medical practitioner has advised an employer that a worker employed by the employer is suffering from health problems which the practitioner considers to be connected with the fact that the worker performs night work, and

(b)   it is possible for the employer to transfer the worker to work—

(i)   to which the worker is suited, and

(ii)   which is to be undertaken during periods such that the worker will cease to be a night worker,

the employer shall transfer the worker accordingly.

8.   Pattern of work

Where the pattern according to which an employer organizes work is such as to put the health and safety of a worker employed by him at risk, in particular because the work is monotonous or the work-rate is predetermined, the employer shall ensure that the worker is given adequate rest breaks.

9.   Records

An employer shall—

(a)   keep records which are adequate to show whether the limits specified in regulations 4(1) and 6(1) and (7) and the requirements in regulations 7(1) and (2) are being complied with in the case of each worker employed by him in relation to whom they apply; and

(b)   retain such records for two years from the date on which they were made.

10.   Daily rest

(1)   An adult worker is entitled to a rest period of not less than eleven consecutive hours in each 24-hour period during which he works for his employer.

(2)   Subject to paragraph (3), a young worker is entitled to a rest period of not less than twelve consecutive hours in each 24-hour period during which he works for his employer.

(3)   The minimum rest period provided for in paragraph (2) may be interrupted in the case of activities involving periods of work that are split up over the day or of short duration.

11.   Weekly rest period

(1)   Subject to paragraph (2), an adult worker is entitled to an uninterrupted rest period of not less than 24 hours in each seven-day period during which he works for his employer.

(2)   If his employer so determines, an adult worker shall be entitled to either—
    (a)   two uninterrupted rest periods each of not less than 24 hours in each 14-day period during which he works for his employer; or
    (b)   one uninterrupted rest period of not less than 48 hours in each such 14-day period, in place of the entitlement provided for in paragraph (1).

(3)   Subject to paragraph (8), a young worker is entitled to a rest period of not less than 48 hours in each seven-day period during which he works for his employer.

(4)   For the purpose of paragraphs (1) to (3), a seven-day period or (as the case may be) 14-day period shall be taken to begin—
    (a)   at such times on such days as may be provided for for the purposes of this regulation in a relevant agreement; or
    (b)   where there are no provisions of a relevant agreement which apply, at the start of each week or (as the case may be) every other week.

(5)   In a case where, in accordance with paragraph (4), 14-day periods are to be taken to begin at the start of every other week, the first such period applicable in the case of a particular worker shall be taken to begin—
    (a)   if the worker's employment began on or before the date on which these Regulations come into force, on 5th October 1998; or
    (b)   if the worker's employment begins after the date on which these Regulations come into force, at the start of the week in which that employment begins.

(6)   For the purposes of paragraphs (4) and (5), a week starts at midnight between Sunday and Monday.

(7)   The minimum rest period to which an adult worker is entitled under paragraph (1) or (2) shall not include any part of a rest period to which the worker is entitled under regulation 10(1), except where this is justified by objective or technical reasons or reasons concerning the organization of work.

(8)   The minimum rest period to which a young worker is entitled under paragraph (3)—
    (a)   may be interrupted in the case of activities involving periods of work that are split up over the day or are of short duration; and
    (b)   may be reduced where this is justified by technical or organization reasons, but not to less than 36 consecutive hours.

12.   Rest breaks

(1)   Where an adult worker's daily working time is more than six hours, he is entitled to a rest break.

(2)   The details of the rest break to which an adult worker is entitled under paragraph (1), including its duration and the terms on which it is granted, shall be in accordance with any provisions for the purposes of this regulation which are contained in a collective agreement or a workforce agreement.

(3)   Subject to the provisions of any applicable collective agreement or workforce agreement, the rest break provided for in paragraph (1) is an uninter-

rupted period of not less than 20 minutes, and the worker is entitled to spend it away from his workstation if he has one.

(4)   Where a young worker's daily working time is more than four and a half hours, he is entitled to a rest break of at least 30 minutes, which shall be consecutive if possible, and he is entitled to spend it away from his workstation if he has one.

(5)   If, on any day, a young worker is employed by more than one employer, his daily working time shall be determined for the purpose of paragraph (4) by aggregating the number of hours worked by him for each employer.

13.   Entitlement to annual leave

(1)   Subject to paragraphs (5) and (7), a worker is entitled in each leave year to a period of leave determined in accordance with paragraph (2).

(2)   The period of leave to which a worker is entitled under paragraph (1) is—

(a)   in any leave year beginning on or before 23rd November 1998, three weeks;

(b)   in any leave year beginning after 23rd November 1998 but before 23rd November 1999, three weeks and a proportion of a fourth week equivalent to the proportion of the year beginning on 23rd November 1998 which has elapsed at the start of that leave year; and

(c)   in any leave year beginning after 23rd November 1999, four weeks.

(3)   A worker's leave year, for the purposes of this regulation, begins—

(a)   on such date during the calendar year as may be provided for in a relevant agreement; or

(b)   where there are no provisions of a relevant agreement which apply—

(i)   if the worker's employment began on or before 1st October 1998, on that date and each subsequent anniversary of that date; or

(ii)   if the worker's employment begins after 1st October 1998, on the date on which that employment begins and each subsequent anniversary of that date.

(4)   Paragraph (3) does not apply to a worker to whom Schedule 2 applies (workers employed in agriculture) except where, in the case of a worker partly employed in agriculture, a relevant agreement so provides.

(5)   Where the date on which a worker's employment begins is later than the date on which (by virtue of a relevant agreement) his first leave year begins, the leave to which he is entitled in that leave year is a proportion of the period applicable under paragraph (2) equal to the proportion of that leave year remaining on the date on which his employment begins.

(6)   Where by virtue of paragraph (2)(b) or (5) the period of leave to which a worker is entitled is or includes a proportion of a week, the proportion shall be determined in days and any fraction of a day shall be treated as a whole day.

(7)   The entitlement conferred by paragraph (1) does not arise until a worker has been continuously employed for thirteen weeks.

(8)   For the purposes of paragraph (7), a worker has been continuously employed for thirteen weeks if his relations with his employer have been governed by a contract during the whole or part of each of those weeks.

(9)   Leave to which a worker is entitled under this regulation may be taken in instalments, but—

(a) it may only be taken in the leave year in respect of which it is due, and

(b) it may not be replaced by a payment in lieu except where the worker's employment is terminated.

14. Compensation related to entitlement to leave

(1) This regulation applies where—

(a) a worker's employment is terminated during the course of his leave year, and

(b) on the date on which the termination takes effect ('the termination date'), the proportion he has taken of the leave to which he is entitled in the leave year under regulation 13(1) differs from the proportion of the leave year which has expired.

(2) Where the proportion of leave taken by the worker is less than the proportion of the leave year which has expired, his employer shall make him a payment in lieu of leave in accordance with paragraph (3).

(3) The payment due under paragraph (2) shall be—

(a) such sum as may be provided for for the purposes of this regulation in a relevant agreement, or

(b) where there are no provisions of a relevant agreement which apply, a sum equal to the amount that would be due to the worker under regulation 16 in respect of a period of leave determined according to the formula—

$$(A \times B) - C$$

where—

A is the period of leave to which the worker is entitled under regulation 13(1);

B is the proportion of the worker's leave year which expired before the termination date, and

C is the period of leave taken by the worker between the start of the leave year and the termination date.

(4) A relevant agreement may provide that, where the proportion of leave taken by the worker exceeds the proportion of the leave year which has expired, he shall compensate his employer, whether by a payment, by undertaking additional work or otherwise.

15. Dates on which leave is taken

(1) A worker may take leave to which he is entitled under regulation 13(1) on such days as he may elect by giving notice to his employer in accordance with paragraph (3), subject to any requirement imposed on him by his employer under paragraph (2).

(2) A worker's employer may require the worker—

(a) to take leave to which the worker is entitled under regulation 13(1); or

(b) not to take such leave,

on particular days, by giving notice to the worker in accordance with paragraph (3).

(3) A notice under paragraph (1) or (2)—

(a) may relate to all or part of the leave to which a worker is entitled in a leave year;

(b) shall specify the days on which leave is or (as the case may be) is not to be taken and, where the leave on a particular day is to be in respect of only part of the day, its duration; and

(c)   shall be given to the employer or, as the case may be, the worker before the relevant date.

(4)   The relevant date, for the purposes of paragraph (3), is the date—

(a)   in the case of a notice under paragraph (1) or (2)(a), twice as many days in advance of the earliest day specified in the notice as the number of days or part-days to which the notice relates, and

(b)   in the case of a notice under paragraph (2)(b), as many days in advance of the earliest day so specified as the number of days or part-days to which the notice relates.

(5)   Any right or obligation under paragraphs (1) to (4) may be varied or excluded by a relevant agreement.

(6)   This regulation does not apply to a worker to whom Schedule 2 applies (workers employed in agriculture) except where, in the case of a worker partly employed in agriculture, a relevant agreement so provides.

16.   Payment in respect of periods of leave

(1)   A worker is entitled to be paid in respect of any period of annual leave to which he is entitled under regulation 13, at the rate of a week's pay in respect of each week of leave.

(2)   Sections 221 to 224 of the 1996 Act shall apply for the purpose of determining the amount of a week's pay for the purposes of this regulation, subject to the modifications set out in paragraph (3).

(3)   The provisions referred to in paragraph (2) shall apply—

(a)   as if references to the employee were references to the worker;

(b)   as if references to the employee's contract of employment were references to the worker's contract;

(c)   as if the calculation date were the first day of the period of leave in question; and

(d)   as if the references to sections 227 and 228 did not apply.

(4)   A right to payment under paragraph (1) does not affect any right of a worker to remuneration under his contract ('contractual remuneration').

(5)   Any contractual remuneration paid to a worker in respect of a period of leave goes towards discharging any liability of the employer to make payments under this regulation in respect of that period; and, conversely, any payment of remuneration under this regulation in respect of a period goes towards discharging any liability of the employer to pay contractual remuneration in respect of that period.

17.   Entitlements under other provisions

Where during any period a worker is entitled to a rest period, rest break or annual leave both under a provision of these Regulations and under a separate provision (including a provision of his contract), he may not exercise the two rights separately, but may, in taking a rest period, break or leave during that period, take advantage of whichever right is, in any particular respect, the more favourable.

PART III
EXCEPTIONS

18.   Excluded sectors

Regulations 4(1) and (2), 6(1), (2) and (7), 7(1), and (6), 8, 10(1), 11 (1) and (2), 12(1), 13 and 16 do not apply—

   (a) to the following sectors of activity—
      (i)   air, rail, road, sea, inland waterway and lake transport;
      (ii) sea fishing;
      (iii) other work at sea; or
   (b) to the activities of doctors in training, or
   (c) where characteristics peculiar to certain specified services such as the armed forces or the police, or to certain specific activities in the civil protection services, inevitably conflict with the provisions of these Regulations.

19. Domestic service

Regulations 4(1) and (2), 6(1), (2) and (7), 7(1), (2) and (6) and 8 do not apply in relation to a worker employed as a domestic servant in a private household.

20. Unmeasured working time

Regulations 4(1) and (2), 6(1), (2) and (7), 10(1), 11 (1) and (2) and 12(1) do not apply in relation to a worker where, on account of the specific characteristics of the activity in which he is engaged, the duration of his working time is not measured or predetermined or can be determined by the worker himself, as may be the case for—
   (a) managing executives or other persons with autonomous decision-taking powers;
   (b) family workers; or
   (c) workers officiating at religious ceremonies in churches and religious communities.

21. Other special cases

Subject to regulation 24, regulations 6(1), (2) and (7), 10(1), 11(1) and (2) and 12(1) do not apply in relation to a worker—
   (a) where the worker's activities are such that his place of work and place of residence are distant from one another or his different places of work are distant from one another;
   (b) where the worker is engaged in security and surveillance activities requiring a permanent presence in order to protect property and persons, as may be the case for security guards and caretakers or security firms;
   (c) where the worker's activities involve the need for continuity of service or production, as may be the case in relation to—
      (i)   services relating to the reception, treatment or care provided by hospitals or similar establishments, residential institutions and prisons;
      (ii) work at docks or airports;
      (iii) press, radio, television, cinematographic production, postal and telecommunications services and civil protection services;
      (iv) gas, water and electricity production, transmission and distribution, household refuse collection and incineration;
      (v) industries in which work cannot be interrupted on technical grounds;
      (vi) research and development activities;
      (vii) agriculture;
   (d) where there is a foreseeable surge of activity, as may be the case in relation to—
      (i)   agriculture;

(ii)   tourism; and

(iii)   postal services;

(e)   where the worker's activities are affected by—

(i)   an occurrence due to unusual and unforeseeable circumstances, beyond the control of the worker's employer;

(ii)   exceptional events, the consequences of which could not have been avoided despite the exercise of all due care by the employer; or

(iii)   an accident or the imminent risk of an accident.

22. Shift workers

(1)   Subject to regulation 24—

(a)   regulation 10(1) does not apply in relation to a shift worker when he changes shift and cannot take a daily rest period between the end of one shift and the start of the next one;

(b)   paragraphs (1) and (2) of regulation 11 do not apply in relation to a shift worker when he changes shift and cannot take a weekly rest period between the end of one shift and the start of the next one; and

(c)   neither regulation 10(1) nor paragraphs (1) and (2) of regulation 11 apply to workers engaged in activities involving periods of work split up over the day, as may be the case for cleaning staff.

(2)   For the purposes of this regulation—

'shift worker' means any worker whose work schedule is part of shift work; and 'shift work' means any method of organizing work in shifts whereby workers succeed each other at the same workstations according to a certain pattern, including a rotating pattern, and which may be continuous or discontinuous, entailing the need for workers to work at different times over a given period of days or weeks.

23. Collective and workforce agreements

A collective agreement or a workforce agreement may—

(a)   modify or exclude the application of regulations 6(1) to (3) and (7), 10(1), 11 (1) and (2) and 12(1), and

(b)   for objective or technical reasons or reasons concerning the organization of work, modify the application of regulation 4(3) and (4) by the substitution, for each reference to 17 weeks, of a different period, being a period not exceeding 52 weeks,

in relation to particular workers or groups of workers.

24. Compensatory rest

Where the application of any provision of these Regulations is excluded by regulation 21 or 22, or is modified or excluded by means of a collective agreement or a workforce agreement under regulation 23(a), and a worker is accordingly required by his employer to work during a period which would otherwise be a rest period or rest break—

(a)   his employer shall wherever possible allow him to take an equivalent period of compensatory rest, and

(b)   in exceptional cases in which it is not possible, for objective reasons, to grant such a period of rest, his employer shall afford him such protection as may be appropriate in order to safeguard the worker's health and safety.

25. Workers in the armed forces

(1)   Regulation 9 does not apply in relation to a worker serving as a member of the armed forces.

(2)   Regulations 10(2) and 11(3) do not apply in relation to a young worker serving as a member of the armed forces.

(3)   In a case where a young worker is accordingly required to work during a period which would otherwise be a rest period, he shall be allowed an appropriate period of compensatory rest.

26. Young workers employed on ships

Regulations 7(2), 10(2), 11(3) and 12(4) do not apply in relation to a young worker whose employment is subject to regulation under section 55(2)(b) of the Merchant Shipping Act 1995.

27. Young workers: *force majeure*

(1)   Regulations 10(2) and 12(4) do not apply in relation to a young worker where his employer requires him to undertake work which no adult worker is available to perform and which—

  (a)   is occasioned by either—

    (i)   an occurrence due to unusual and unforeseeable circumstances, beyond the employer's control, or

    (ii)   exceptional events, the consequences of which could not have been avoided despite the exercise of all due care by the employer;

  (b)   is of a temporary nature; and

  (c)   must be performed immediately.

(2)   Where the application of regulation 10(2) or 12(4) is excluded by paragraph (1), and a young worker is accordingly required to work during a period which would otherwise be a rest period or rest break, his employer shall allow him to take an equivalent period of compensatory rest within the following three weeks.

PART IV
MISCELLANEOUS

28. Enforcement

(1)   In this regulation and regulation 29—

'the 1974 Act' means the Health and Safety at Work etc. Act 1974;

'the relevant requirements' means the following provisions—

  (a)   regulations 4(2), 6(2) and (7), 7(1), (2) and (6), 8 and 9; and

  (b)   regulation 24, in so far as it applies where regulation 6(1), (2) or (7) is modified or excluded, and

'the relevant statutory provisions' has the same meaning as in the 1974 Act.

(2)   It shall be the duty of the Health and Safety Executive to make adequate arrangements for the enforcement of the relevant requirements except to the extent that a local authority is made responsible for their enforcement by paragraph (3).

(3)   Where the relevant requirements apply in relation to workers employed in premises in respect of which a local authority is responsible, under the Health and Safety (Enforcing Authority) Regulations 1998, for enforcing any of the relevant statutory provisions, it shall be the duty of that authority to enforce those requirements.

(4)   The duty imposed on local authorities by paragraph (3) shall be performed in accordance with such guidance as may be given to them by the Health and Safety Commission.

(5)   The following provisions of the 1974 Act shall apply in relation to the enforcement of the relevant requirements as they apply in relation to the enforcement of the relevant statutory provisions, and as if any reference in those provisions to an enforcing authority were a reference to the Health and Safety Executive and any local authority made responsible for the enforcement of the relevant requirements—

(a)   section 19;

(b)   section 20(1), (2)(a) to (d) and (j) to (m), (7) and (8); and

(c)   sections 21, 22, 23(1), (2) and (5), 24 and 26; and

(d)   section 28, in so far as it relates to information obtained by an inspector in pursuance of a requirement imposed under section 20(2)(j) or (k).

(6)   Any function of the Health and Safety Commission under the 1974 Act which is exercisable in relation to the enforcement by the Health and Safety Executive of the relevant statutory provisions shall be exercisable in relation to the enforcement by the Executive of the relevant requirements.

29. Offences

(1)   An employer who fails to comply with any of the relevant requirements shall be guilty of an offence.

(2)   The following provisions of section 33(1) of the 1974 Act shall apply where an inspector is exercising or has exercised any power conferred by a provision specified in regulation 28(5)—

(a)   paragraph (e), in so far as it refers to section 20;

(b)   paragraphs (f) and (g);

(c)   paragraph (h), in so far as it refers to an inspector;

(d)   paragraph (j) in so far as it refers to section 28; and

(e)   paragraph (k).

(3)   An employer guilty of an offence under paragraph (1) shall be liable—

(a)   on summary conviction, to a fine not exceeding the statutory maximum;

(b)   on conviction on indictment, to a fine.

(4)   A person guilty of an offence under a provision of section 33(1) of the 1974 Act as applied by paragraph (2) shall be liable to the penalty prescribed in relation to that provision by subsection (2), (2A) or (3) of section 33, as the case may be.

(5)   Sections 36(1), 37 to 39 and 42(1) to (3) of the 1974 Act shall apply in relation to the offences provided for in paragraphs (1) and (2) as they apply in relation to offences under the relevant statutory provisions.

30. Remedies

(1)   A worker may present a complaint to an employment tribunal that his employer—

(a)   has refused to permit him to exercise any right he has under—

(i)   regulation 10(1) or (2), 11(1), (2) or (3), 12(1) or (4) or 13(1);

(ii)   regulation 24, in so far as it applies where regulation 10(1), 11(1) or (2) or 12(1) is modified or excluded; or

(iii)   regulation 25(3) or 27(2); or

(b)   has failed to pay him the whole or any part of any amount due to him under regulation 14(2) or 16(1).

(2)   An employment tribunal shall not consider a complaint under this regulation unless it is presented—

(a)   before the end of the period of three months (or, in a case to which regulation 38(2) applies, six months) beginning with the date on which it is alleged that the exercise of the right should have been permitted (or in the case of a rest period or leave extending over more than one day, the date on which it should have been permitted to begin) or, as the case may be, the payment should have been made;

(b)   within such further period as the tribunal considers reasonable in a case where it is satisfied that it was not reasonably practicable for the complaint to be presented before the end of that period of three or, as the case may be, six months.

(3)   Where an employment tribunal finds a complaint under paragraph (1)(a) well-founded, the tribunal—

(a)   shall make a declaration to that effect, and

(b)   may make an award of compensation to be paid by the employer to the worker.

(4)   The amount of the compensation shall be such as the tribunal considers just and equitable in all the circumstances having regard to—

(a)   the employer's default in refusing to permit the worker to exercise his right, and

(b)   any loss sustained by the worker which is attributable to the matters complained of.

(5)   Where on a complaint under paragraph (1)(b) an employment tribunal finds that an employer has failed to pay a worker in accordance with regulation 14(2) or 16(1), it shall order the employer to pay to the worker the amount which it finds to be due to him.

31.   Right not to suffer detriment

(1)   After section 45 of the 1996 Act there shall be inserted—

'45A.   Working time cases

(1)   A worker has the right not to be subjected to any detriment by any act, or any deliberate failure to act, by his employer done on the ground that the worker—

(a)   refused (or proposed to refuse) to comply with a requirement which the employer imposed (or proposed to impose) in contravention of the Working Time Regulations 1998,

(b)   refused (or proposed to refuse) to forgo a right conferred on him by those Regulations,

(c)   failed to sign a workforce agreement for the purposes of those Regulations, or to enter into, or agree to vary or extend, any other agreement with his employer which is provided for in those Regulations,

(d)   being—

(i)   a representative of members of the workforce for the purposes of Schedule 1 to those Regulations, or

(ii)   a candidate in an election in which any person elected will, on being elected, be such a representative,

performed (or proposed to perform) any functions or activities as such a representative or candidate,

(e) brought proceedings against the employer to enforce a right conferred on him by those Regulations, or

(f) alleged that the employer had infringed such a right.

(2) It is immaterial for the purposes of subsection (1)(e) or (f)—

(a) whether or not the worker has the right, or

(b) whether or not the right has been infringed,

but, for those provisions to apply, the claim to the right and that it has been infringed must be made in good faith.

(3) It is sufficient for subsection (1)(f) to apply that the worker, without specifying the right, made it reasonably clear to the employer what the right claimed to have been infringed was.

(4) This section does not apply where a worker is an employee and the detriment in question amounts to dismissal within the meaning of Part X, unless the dismissal is in circumstances in which, by virtue of section 197, Part X does not apply.'

(2) After section 48(1) of the 1996 Act there shall be inserted the following subsection—

'(1ZA) A worker may present a complaint to an employment tribunal that he has been subjected to a detriment in contravention of section 45A.'

(3) In section 49 of the 1996 Act (remedies)—

(a) in subsection (2), for 'subsection (6)' there shall be substituted 'subsections (5A) and (6)', and

(b) after subsection (5), there shall be inserted—

'(5A) Where—

(a) the complaint is made under section 48(1ZA),

(b) the detriment to which the worker is subjected is the termination of his worker's contract, and

(c) that contract is not a contract of employment,

any compensation must not exceed the compensation that would be payable under Chapter II of Part X if the worker had been an employee and had been dismissed for the reason specified in section 101A.'

(4) In section 192(2) of the 1996 Act (provisions applicable in relation to service in the armed forces), after paragraph (a) there shall be inserted—

'(aa) in Part V, section 45A, and sections 48 and 49 so far as relating to that section,'.

(5) In sections 194(2)(c), 195(2)(c) and 202(2)(b) of the 1996 Act, for 'sections 44 and 47' there shall be substituted 'sections 44, 45A and 47'.

(6) In section 200(1) of the 1996 Act (which lists provisions of the Act which do not apply to employment in police service), after '45,' there shall be inserted '45A,'.

(7) In section 205 of the 1996 Act (remedy for infringement of certain rights), after subsection (1) there shall be inserted the following subsection—

'(1ZA) In relation to the right conferred by section 45A, the reference in subsection (1) to an employee has effect as a reference to a worker.'

32. Unfair dismissal

(1) After section 101 of the 1996 Act there shall be inserted the following section—

'101A. Working time cases

An employee who is dismissed shall be regarded for the purposes of this Part as unfairly dismissed if the reason (or, if more than one, the principal reason) for the dismissal is that the employee—

(a)   refused (or proposed to refuse) to comply with a requirement which the employer imposed (or proposed to impose) in contravention of the Working Time Regulations 1998,

(b)   refused (or proposed to refuse) to forgo a right conferred on him by those Regulations,

(c)   failed to sign a workforce agreement for the purposes of those Regulations, or to enter into, or agree to vary or extend, any other agreement with his employer which is provided for in those Regulations, or

(d)   being—

(i)   a representative of members of the workforce for the purposes of Schedule 1 to those Regulations, or

(ii)   a candidate in an election in which any person elected will, on being elected, be such a representative,

performed (or proposed to perform) any functions or activities as such a representative or candidate.'

(2)   In section 104 of the 1996 Act (right of employees not to be unfairly dismissed for asserting particular rights) in subsection (4)—

(a)   at the end of paragraph (b), the word 'and' shall be omitted, and

(b)   after paragraph (c), there shall be inserted the words—

'and

(d)   the rights conferred by the Working Time Regulations 1998.'

(3)   In section 105 of the 1996 Act (redundancy as unfair dismissal), after subsection (4) there shall be inserted the following subsection—

'(4A)   This subsection applies if the reason (or, if more than one, the principal reason) for which the employee was selected for dismissal was one of those specified in section 101A.'

(4)   In sections 108(3) and 109(2) of the 1996 Act, after paragraph (d) there shall be inserted—

'(dd)   section 101A applies,'.

(5)   In sections 117(4)(b), 118(3), 120(1), 122(3), 128(1)(b) and 129(1) of the 1996 Act, after '100(1)(a) and (b),' there shall be inserted '101A(d),'.

(6)   In section 202(2) (cases where disclosure of information is restricted on ground of national security)—

(a)   in paragraph (g)(i), after '100' there shall be inserted ', 101A(d)', and

(b)   in paragraph (g)(ii), after 'of that section,' there shall be inserted 'or by reason of the application of subsection (4A) in so far as it applies where the reason (or, if more than one, the principal reason) for which an employee was selected for dismissal was that specified in section 101A(d)'.

(7)   In section 209(2) of the 1996 Act (which lists provisions excluded from the scope of the power to amend the Act by order), after '101,' in paragraph (e) there shall be inserted '101A,'.

(8)   In sections 237(1A) and 238(2A) of the Trade Union and Labour Relations (Consolidation) Act 1992 (cases where employee can complain of unfair dismissal

notwithstanding industrial action at time of dismissal), after '100' there shall be inserted ', 101A(d)'.

(9)   In section 10(5)(a) of the Employment Tribunals Act 1996 (cases where Minister's certificate is not conclusive evidence that action was taken to safeguard national security), after '100' there shall be inserted ', 101A(d)'.

33.   Conciliation
In section 18(1) of the Employment Tribunals Act 1996 (cases where conciliation provisions apply)—

(a)   at the end of paragraph (e), the word 'or' shall be omitted, and

(b)   after paragraph (f), there shall be inserted the words—

'or

(ff) under regulation 30 of the Working Time Regulations 1998,'.

34.   Appeals
In section 21 of the Employment Tribunals Act 1996 (jurisdiction of the Employment Appeal Tribunal)—

(a)   at the end of subsection (1) (which confers jurisdiction by reference to Acts under or by virtue of which decisions are made) there shall be inserted—

'or under the Working Time Regulations 1998.';

(b)   in subsection (2), after 'the Acts listed' there shall be inserted—

'or the Regulations referred to'.

35.   Restrictions on contracting out
(1)   Any provision in an agreement (whether a contract of employment or not) is void in so far as it purports—

(a)   to exclude or limit the operation of any provision of these Regulations, save in so far as these Regulations provide for an agreement to have that effect, or

(b)   to preclude a person from bringing proceedings under these Regulations before an employment tribunal.

(2)   Paragraph (1) does not apply to—

(a)   any agreement to refrain from instituting or continuing proceedings where a conciliation officer has taken action under section 18 of the Employment Tribunals Act 1996 (conciliation); or

(b)   any agreement to refrain from instituting or continuing proceedings within section 18(1)(ff) of the Employment Tribunals Act 1996 (proceedings under these Regulations where conciliation is available), if the conditions regulating compromise agreements under these Regulations are satisfied in relation to the agreement.

(3)   For the purposes of paragraph (2)(b) the conditions regulating compromise agreements under these Regulations are that—

(a)   the agreement must be in writing,

(b)   the agreement must relate to the particular complaint,

(c)   the worker must have received advice from a relevant independent adviser as to the terms and effect of the proposed agreement and, in particular, its effect on his ability to pursue his rights before an employment tribunal,

(d)   there must be in force, when the adviser gives the advice, a contract of insurance, or an indemnity provided for members of a profession or professional body, covering the risk of a claim by the worker in respect of loss arising in consequence of the advice,

(e) the agreement must identify the adviser, and

(f) the agreement must state that the conditions regulating compromise agreements under these Regulations are satisfied.

(4) A person is a relevant independent adviser for the purposes of paragraph (3)(c)—

(a) if he is a qualified lawyer,

(b) if he is an officer, official, employee or member of an independent trade union who has been certified in writing by the trade union as competent to give advice and as authorised to do so on behalf of the trade union, or

(c) if he works at an advice centre (whether as an employee or as a volunteer) and has been certified in writing by the centre as competent to give advice and as authorised to do so on behalf of the centre.

(5) But a person is not a relevant independent adviser for the purposes of paragraph (3)(c) in relation to the worker—

(a) if he is, is employed by or is acting in the matter for the employer or an associated employer,

(b) in the case of a person within paragraph (4)(b) or (c), if the trade union or advice centre is the employer or an associated employer, or

(c) in the case of a person within paragraph (4)(c), if the worker makes a payment for the advice received from him.

(6) In paragraph (4)(a), 'qualified lawyer' means—

(a) as respects England and Wales, a barrister (whether in practice as such or employed to give legal advice), a solicitor who holds a practising certificate, or a person other than a barrister or solicitor who is an authorised advocate or authorised litigator (within the meaning of the Courts and Legal Services Act 1990); and

(b) as respects Scotland, an advocate (whether in practice as such or employed to give legal advice), or a solicitor who holds a practising certificate.

(7) For the purposes of paragraph (5) any two employers shall be treated as associated if—

(a) one is a company of which the other (directly or indirectly) has control; or

(b) both are companies of which a third person (directly or indirectly) has control;

and 'associated employer' shall be construed accordingly.

PART V
SPECIAL CLASSES OF PERSON

36. Agency workers not otherwise 'workers'

(1) This regulation applies in any case where an individual ('the agency worker')—

(a) is supplied by a person ('the agent') to do work for another ('the principal') under a contract or other arrangements made between the agent and the principal; but

(b) is not, as respects that work, a worker, because of the absence of a worker's contract between the individual and the agent or the principal; and

(c) is not a party to a contract under which he undertakes to do the work for another party to the contract whose status is, by virtue of the contract, that of a client or customer of any profession or business undertaking carried on by the individual.

(2) In a case where this regulation applies, the other provisions of these Regulations shall have effect as if there were a worker's contract for the doing of the work by the agency worker made between the agency worker and—

(a) whichever of the agent and the principal is responsible for paying the agency worker in respect of the work; or

(b) if neither the agent nor the principal is so responsible, whichever of them pays the agency worker in respect of the work,

and as if that person were the agency worker's employer.

37. Crown employment

(1) Subject to paragraph (4) and regulation 38, these Regulations have effect in relation to Crown employment and persons in Crown employment as they have effect in relation to other employment and other workers.

(2) In paragraph (1) 'Crown employment' means employment under or for the purposes of a government department or any officer or body exercising on behalf of the Crown functions conferred by a statutory provision.

(3) For the purposes of the application of the provisions of these Regulations in relation to Crown employment in accordance with paragraph (1)—

(a) references to a worker shall be construed as references to a person in Crown employment; and

(b) references to a worker's contract shall be construed as references to the terms of employment of a person in Crown employment.

(4) No act or omission by the Crown which is an offence under regulation 29 shall make the Crown criminally liable, but the High Court or, in Scotland, the Court of Session may, on the application of a person appearing to the Court to have an interest, declare any such act or omission unlawful.

38. Armed forces

(1) Regulation 37 applies—

(a) subject to paragraph (2), to service as a member of the armed forces, and

(b) to employment by an association established for the purposes of Part XI of the Reserve Forces Act 1996.

(2) No complaint concerning the service of any person as a member of the armed forces may be presented to an employment tribunal under regulation 30 unless—

(a) that person has made a complaint in respect of the same matter to an officer under the service redress procedures, and

(b) that complaint has not been withdrawn.

(3) For the purposes of paragraph (2)(b), a person shall be treated as having withdrawn his complaint if, having made a complaint to an officer under the service redress procedures, he fails to submit the complaint to the Defence Council under those procedures.

(4) Where a complaint of the kind referred to in paragraph (2) is presented to an employment tribunal, the service redress procedures may continue after the complaint is presented.

(5) In this regulation, 'the service redress procedures' means the procedures, excluding those which relate to the making of a report on a complaint to Her

Majesty, referred to in section 180 of the Army Act 1955, section 180 of the Air Force Act 1955 and section 130 of the Naval Discipline Act 1957.

39. House of Lords staff

(1) These Regulations have effect in relation to employment as a relevant member of the House of Lords staff as they have effect in relation to other employment.

(2) Nothing in any rule of law or the law or practice of Parliament prevents a relevant member of the House of Lords staff from presenting a complaint to an employment tribunal under regulation 30.

(3) In this regulation 'relevant member of the House of Lords staff' means any person who is employed under a worker's contract with the Corporate Officer of the House of Lords.

40. House of Commons staff

(1) These Regulations have effect in relation to employment as a relevant member of the House of Commons staff as they have effect in relation to other employment.

(2) For the purposes of the application of the provisions of these Regulations in relation to a relevant member of the House of Commons staff—

(a) references to a worker shall be construed as references to a relevant member of the House of Commons staff; and

(b) references to a worker's contract shall be construed as references to the terms of employment of a relevant member of the House of Commons staff.

(3) Nothing in any rule of law or the law or practice of Parliament prevents a relevant member of the House of Commons staff from presenting a complaint to an employment tribunal under regulation 30.

(4) In this regulation 'relevant member of the House of Commons staff' means any person—

(a) who was appointed by the House of Commons Commission; or

(b) who is a member of the Speaker's personal staff.

41. Police service

(1) For the purposes of these Regulations, the holding, otherwise than under a contract of employment, of the office of constable or an appointment as a police cadet shall be treated as employment, under a worker's contract, by the relevant officer.

(2) Any matter relating to the employment of a worker which may be provided for for the purposes of these Regulations in a workforce agreement may be provided for for the same purposes in relation to the service of a person holding the office of constable or an appointment as a police cadet by an agreement between the relevant officer and a joint branch board.

(3) In this regulation—

'a joint branch board' means a joint branch board constituted in accordance with regulation 7(3) of the Police Federation Regulations 1969 or regulation 7(3) of the Police Federation (Scotland) Regulations 1985, and

'the relevant officer' means—

(a) in relation to a member of a police force or a special constable or police cadet appointed for a police area, the chief officer of police (or, in Scotland, the chief constable);

(b)   in relation to a person holding office under section 9(1)(b) or 55(1)(b) of the Police Act 1997 (police members of the National Criminal Intelligence Service and the National Crime Squad), the Director General of the National Criminal Intelligence Service or, as the case may be, the Director General of the National Crime Squad; and

(c)   in relation to any other person holding the office of constable or an appointment as a police cadet, the person who has the direction and control of the body of constables or cadets in question.

42.   Non-employed trainees

For the purposes of these Regulations, a person receiving relevant training, otherwise than under a contract of employment, shall be regarded as a worker, and the person whose undertaking is providing the training shall be regarded as his employer.

43.   Agricultural workers

The provisions of Schedule 2 have effect in relation to workers employed in agriculture.

Ian McCartney
Minister of State,
30th July 1998   Department of Trade and Industry

SCHEDULE 1   Regulation 2
WORKFORCE AGREEMENTS

1.   An agreement is a workforce agreement for the purposes of these Regulations if the following conditions are satisfied—

(a)   the agreement is in writing;

(b)   it has effect for a specified period not exceeding five years;

(c)   it applies either—

(i)   to all of the relevant members of the workforce, or

(ii)   to all of the relevant members of the workforce who belong to a particular group;

(d)   the agreement is signed—

(i)   in the case of an agreement of the kind referred to in sub-paragraph (c)(i), by the representatives of the workforce, and in the case of an agreement of the kind referred to in sub-paragraph (c)(ii) by the representatives of the group to which the agreement applies (excluding, in either case, any representative not a relevant member of the workforce on the date on which the agreement was first made available for signature), or

(ii)   if the employer employed 20 or fewer workers on the date referred to in sub-paragraph (d)(i), either by the appropriate representatives in accordance with that sub-paragraph or by the majority of the workers employed by him;

(e)   before the agreement was made available for signature, the employer provided all the workers to whom it was intended to apply on the date on which it came into effect with copies of the text of the agreement and such guidance as those workers might reasonably require in order to understand it fully.

2.   For the purposes of this Schedule—

'a particular group' is a group of the relevant members of a workforce who undertake a particular function, work at a particular workplace or belong to a particular department or unit within their employer's business;
'relevant members of the workforce' are all of the workers employed by a particular employer, excluding any worker whose terms and conditions of employment are provided for, wholly or in part, in a collective agreement;
'representatives of the workforce' are workers duly elected to represent the relevant members of the workforce, 'representatives of the group' are workers duly elected to represent the members of a particular group, and representatives are 'duly elected' if the election at which they were elected satisfied the requirements of paragraph 3 of this Schedule.

3.   The requirements concerning elections referred to in paragraph 2 are that—
   (a)   the number of representatives to be elected is determined by the employer;
   (b)   the candidates for election as representatives of the workforce are relevant members of the workforce, and the candidates for election as representatives of a group are members of the group;
   (c)   no worker who is eligible to be a candidate is unreasonably excluded from standing for election;
   (d)   all the relevant members of the workforce are entitled to vote for representatives of the workforce, and all the members of a particular group are entitled to vote for representatives of the group;
   (e)   the workers entitled to vote may vote for as many candidates as there are representatives to be elected;
   (f)   the election is conducted so as to secure that—
      (i)   so far as is reasonably practicable, those voting do so in secret, and
      (ii)   the votes given at the election are fairly and accurately counted.

SCHEDULE 2   Regulations 13(4), 15(6) and 43
WORKERS EMPLOYED IN AGRICULTURE

1.   Except where, in the case of a worker partly employed in agriculture, different provision is made by a relevant agreement—
   (a)   for the purposes of regulation 13, the leave year of a worker employed in agriculture begins on 6th April each year or such other date as may be specified in an agricultural wages order which applies to him; and
   (b)   the dates on which leave is taken by a worker employed in agriculture shall be determined in accordance with an agricultural wages order which applies to him.

2.   Where, in the case referred to in paragraph 1 above, a relevant agreement makes provision different from sub-paragraph (a) or (b) of that paragraph—
   (a)   neither section 11 of the Agricultural Wages Act 1948 nor section 11 of the Agricultural Wages (Scotland) Act 1949 shall apply to that provision; and
   (b)   an employer giving effect to that provision shall not thereby be taken to have failed to comply with the requirements of an agricultural wages order.

3.   In this Schedule, 'an agricultural wages order' means an order under section 3 of the Agricultural Wages Act 1948 or section 3 of the Agricultural Wages (Scotland) Act 1949.

KING'S COLLEGE LONDON LIBRARY

Appendix Two
Text of the Working Time Directive

Council Directive 93/104/EC
of 23 November 1993
concerning certain aspects of the organization of working time

THE COUNCIL OF THE EUROPEAN UNION,

Having regard to the Treaty establishing the European Community, and in particular Article 118a thereof,

Having regard to the proposal from the Commission,

In cooperation with the European Parliament,

Having regard to the opinion of the Economic and Social Committee,

Whereas Article 118a of the Treaty provides that the Council shall adopt, by means of Directives, minimum requirements for encouraging improvements, especially in the working environment, to ensure a better level of protection of the safety and health of workers;

Whereas, under the terms of that Article, those Directives are to avoid imposing administrative, financial and legal constraints in a way which would hold back the creation and development of small and medium-sized undertakings;

Whereas the provisions of Council Directive 89/391/EEC of 12 June 1989 on the introduction of measures to encourage improvements in the safety and health of workers at work are fully applicable to the areas covered by this Directive without prejudice to more stringent and/or specific provisions contained therein;

Whereas the Community Charter of the Fundamental Social Rights of Workers, adopted at the meeting of the European Council held at Strasbourg on 9 December 1989 by the Heads of State or of Government of 11 Member States, and in particular points 7, first subparagraph, 8 and 19, first subparagraph, thereof, declared that:

'7.   The completion of the internal market must lead to an improvement in the living and working conditions of workers in the European Community. This process must result from an approximation of these conditions while the improvement is being maintained, as regards in particular the duration and organization of working time and forms of employment other than open-ended contracts, such as fixed-term contracts, part-time working, temporary work and seasonal work.

8.   Every worker in the European Community shall have a right to a weekly rest period and to annual paid leave, the duration of which must be progressively harmonized in accordance with national practices.

19.   Every worker must enjoy satisfactory health and safety conditions in his working environment. Appropriate measures must be taken in order to achieve further harmonization of conditions in this area while maintaining the improvements made.';

Whereas the improvement of workers' safety, hygiene and health at work is an objective which should not be subordinated to purely economic considerations;

Whereas this Directive is a practical contribution towards creating the social dimension of the internal market;

Whereas laying down minimum requirements with regard to the organization of working time is likely to improve the working conditions of workers in the Community;

Whereas, in order to ensure the safety and health of Community workers, the latter must be granted minimum daily, weekly and annual periods of rest and adequate breaks; whereas it is also necessary in this context to place a maximum limit on weekly working hours;

Whereas account should be taken of the principles of the International Labour Organization with regard to the organization of working time, including those relating to night work;

Whereas, with respect to the weekly rest period, due account should be taken of the diversity of cultural, ethnic, religious and other factors in the Member States; whereas, in particular, it is ultimately for each Member State to decide whether Sunday should be included in the weekly rest period, and if so to what extent;

Whereas research has shown that the human body is more sensitive at night to environmental disturbances and also to certain burdensome forms of work organization and that long periods of night work can be detrimental to the health of workers and can endanger safety at the workplace;

Whereas there is a need to limit the duration of periods of night work, including overtime, and to provide for employers who regularly use night workers to bring this information to the attention of the competent authorities if they so request;

Whereas it is important that night workers should be entitled to a free health assessment prior to their assignment and thereafter at regular intervals and that whenever possible they should be transferred to day work for which they are suited if they suffer from health problems;

Whereas the situation of night and shift workers requires that the level of safety and health protection should be adapted to the nature of their work and that the organization and functioning of protection and prevention services and resources should be efficient;

Whereas specific working conditions may have detrimental effects on the safety and health of workers; whereas the organization of work according to a certain pattern must take account of the general principle of adapting work to the worker;

Whereas, given the specific nature of the work concerned, it may be necessary to adopt separate measures with regard to the organization of working time in certain sectors or activities which are excluded from the scope of this Directive;

Whereas, in view of the question likely to be raised by the organization of working time within an undertaking, it appears desirable to provide for flexibility in the application of certain provisions of this Directive, whilst ensuring compliance with the principles of protecting the safety and health of workers;

Whereas it is necessary to provide that certain provisions may be subject to derogations implemented, according to the case, by the Member States or the two sides of industry; whereas, as a general rule, in the event of a derogation, the workers concerned must be given equivalent compensatory rest periods,

HAS ADOPTED THIS DIRECTIVE:

SECTION I
SCOPE AND DEFINITIONS

Article 1

Purpose and scope

1. This Directive lays down minimum safety and health requirements for the organization of working time.

2. This Directive applies to:

(a) minimum periods of daily rest, weekly rest and annual leave, to breaks and maximum weekly working time; and

(b) certain aspects of night work, shift work and patterns of work.

3. This Directive shall apply to all sectors of activity, both public and private, within the meaning of Article 2 of Directive 89/391/EEC, without prejudice to Article 17 of this Directive, with the exception of air, rail, road, sea, inland waterway and lake transport, sea fishing, other work at sea and the activities of doctors in training;

4. The provisions of Directive 89/391/EEC are fully applicable to the matters referred to in paragraph 2, without prejudice to more stringent and/or specific provisions contained in this Directive.

Article 2

Definitions

For the purposes of this Directive, the following definitions shall apply:

1. *working time* shall mean any period during which the worker is working, at the employer's disposal and carrying out his activity or duties, in accordance with national laws and/or practice;

2. *rest period* shall mean any period which is not working time;

3. *night time* shall mean any period of not less than seven hours, as defined by national law, and which must include in any case the period between midnight and 5 a.m.;

4. *night worker* shall mean:

(a) on the one hand, any worker, who, during night time, works at least three hours of his daily working time as a normal course; and

(b) on the other hand, any worker who is likely during night time to work a certain proportion of his annual working time, as defined at the choice of the Member State concerned:

(i) by national legislation, following consultation with the two sides of industry; or

(ii) by collective agreements or agreements concluded between the two sides of industry at national or regional level;

5. *shift work* shall mean any method of organizing work in shifts whereby workers succeed each other at the same work stations according to a certain pattern, including a rotating pattern, and which may be continuous or discontinuous, entailing the need for workers to work at different times over a given period of days or weeks;

6. *shift worker* shall mean any worker whose work schedule is part of shift work.

SECTION II
MINIMUM REST PERIODS — OTHER ASPECTS OF THE ORGANIZATION OF WORKING TIME

Article 3

Daily rest

Member States shall take the measures necessary to ensure that every worker is entitled to a minimum daily rest period of 11 consecutive hours per 24-hour period.

Article 4

Breaks

Member States shall take the measures necessary to ensure that, where the working day is longer than six hours, every worker is entitled to a rest break, the details of which, including duration and the terms on which it is granted, shall be laid down in collective agreements or agreements between the two sides of industry or, failing that, by national legislation.

Article 5

Weekly rest period

Member States shall take the measures necessary to ensure that, per each seven-day period, every worker is entitled to a minimum uninterrupted rest period of 24 hours plus the 11 hours' daily rest referred to in Article 3.

The minimum rest period referred to in the first subparagraph shall in principle include Sunday.

If objective, technical or work organization conditions so justify, a minimum rest period of 24 hours may be applied.

Article 6

Maximum weekly working time

Member States shall take the measures necessary to ensure that, in keeping with the need to protect the safety and health of workers:

1. the period of weekly working time is limited by means of laws, regulations or administrative provisions or by collective agreements or agreements between the two sides of industry;

2. the average working time for each seven-day period, including overtime, does not exceed 48 hours.

Article 7

Annual leave

1. Member States shall take the measures necessary to ensure that every worker is entitled to paid annual leave of at least four weeks in accordance with

the conditions for entitlement to, and granting of, such leave laid down by national legislation and/or practice.

2.   The minimum period of paid annual leave may not be replaced by an allowance in lieu, except where the employment relationship is terminated.

SECTION III
NIGHT WORK — SHIFT WORK — PATTERNS OF WORK

Article 8

Length of night work

Member States shall take the measures necessary to ensure that:

1.   normal hours of work for night workers do not exceed an average of eight hours in any 24-hour period;

2.   night workers whose work involves special hazards or heavy physical or mental strain do not work more than eight hours in any period of 24 hours during which they perform night work.

For the purposes of the aforementioned, work involving special hazards or heavy physical or mental strain shall be defined by national legislation and/or practice or by collective agreements or agreements concluded between the two sides of industry, taking account of the specific effects and hazards of night work.

Article 9

Health assessment and transfer of night workers to day work

1.   Member States shall take the measures necessary to ensure that:

   (a)   night workers are entitled to a free health assessment before their assignment and thereafter at regular intervals;

   (b)   night workers suffering from health problems recognized as being connected with the fact that they perform night work are transferred whenever possible to day work to which they are suited.

2.   The free health assessment referred to in paragraph 1(a) must comply with medical confidentiality.

3.   The free health assessment referred to in paragraph 1(a) may be conducted within the national health system.

Article 10

Guarantees for night-time working

Member States may make the work of certain categories of night workers subject to certain guarantees, under conditions laid down by national legislation and/or practice, in the case of workers who incur risks to their safety or health linked to night-time working.

Article 11

Notification of regular use of night workers

Member States shall take the measures necessary to ensure that an employer who regularly uses night workers brings this information to the attention of the competent authorities if they so request.

Article 12

Safety and health protection

Member States shall take the measures necessary to ensure that:

1. night workers and shift workers have safety and health protection appropriate to the nature of their work;

2. appropriate protection and prevention services or facilities with regard to the safety and health of night workers and shift workers are equivalent to those applicable to other workers and are available at all times.

Article 13

Pattern of work

Member States shall take the measures necessary to ensure that an employer who intends to organize work according to a certain pattern takes account of the general principle of adapting work to the worker, with a view, in particular, to alleviating monotonous work and work at a predetermined work-rate, depending on the type of activity, and of safety and health requirements, especially as regards breaks during working time.

SECTION IV
MISCELLANEOUS PROVISIONS

Article 14

More specific Community provisions

The provisions of this Directive shall not apply where other Community instruments contain more specific requirements concerning certain occupations or occupational activities.

Article 15

More favourable provisions

This Directive shall not affect Member States' right to apply or introduce laws, regulations or administrative provisions more favourable to the protection of the safety and health of workers or to facilitate or permit the application of collective agreements or agreements concluded between the two sides of industry which are more favourable to the protection of the safety and health of workers.

Article 16

Reference periods

Member States may lay down:

1. for the application of Article 5 (weekly rest period), a reference period not exceeding 14 days;

2. for the application of Article 6 (maximum weekly working time), a reference period not exceeding four months.

The periods of paid annual leave, granted in accordance with Article 7, and the periods of sick leave shall not be included or shall be neutral in the calculation of the average;

3. for the application of Article 8 (length of night work), a reference period defined after consultation of the two sides of industry or by collective agreements or agreements concluded between the two sides of industry at national or regional level.

If the minimum weekly rest period of 24 hours required by Article 5 falls within that reference period, it shall not be included in the calculation of the average.

Article 17

Derogations

1. With due regard for the general principles of the protection of the safety and health of workers, Member States may derogate from Article 3, 4, 5, 6, 8 or 16 when, on account of the specific characteristics of the activity concerned, the duration of the working time is not measured and/or predetermined or can be determined by the workers themselves, and particularly in the case of:

    (a) managing executives or other persons with autonomous decision-taking powers;

    (b) family workers; or

    (c) workers officiating at religious ceremonies in churches and religious communities.

2. Derogations may be adopted by means of laws, regulations or administrative provisions or by means of collective agreements or agreements between the two sides of industry provided that the workers concerned are afforded equivalent periods of compensatory rest or that, in exceptional cases in which it is not possible, for objective reasons, to grant such equivalent periods of compensatory rest, the workers concerned are afforded appropriate protection:

2.1 from Articles 3, 4, 5, 8 and 16:

    (a) in the case of activities where the worker's place of work and his place of residence are distant from one another or where the worker's different places of work are distant from one another;

    (b) in the case of security and surveillance activities requiring a permanent presence in order to protect property and persons, particularly security guards and caretakers or security firms;

    (c) in the case of activities involving the need for continuity of service or production, particularly:

        (i) services relating to the reception, treatment and/or care provided by hospitals or similar establishments, residential institutions and prisons;

        (ii) dock or airport workers;

        (iii) press, radio, television, cinematographic production, postal and tele-communications services, ambulance, fire and civil protection services;

        (iv) gas, water and electricity production, transmission and distribution, household refuse collection and incineration plants;

        (v) industries in which work cannot be interrupted on technical grounds;

        (vi) research and development activities;

        (vii) agriculture;

    (d) where there is a foreseeable surge of activity, particularly in:

        (i) agriculture;

        (ii) tourism;

        (iii) postal services;

2.2. from Articles 3, 4, 5, 8 and 16:

(a)   in the circumstances described in Article 5(4) of Directive 89/391/EEC;

(b)   in cases of accident or imminent risk of accident;

2.3   from Articles 3 and 5:

(a)   in the case of shift work activities, each time the worker changes shift and cannot take daily and/or weekly rest periods between the end of one shift and the start of the next one;

(b)   in the case of activities involving periods of work split up over the day, particularly those of cleaning staff.

3.   Derogations may be made from Articles 3, 4, 5, 8 and 16 by means of collective agreements or agreements concluded between the two sides of industry at national or regional level or, in conformity with the rules laid down by them, by means of collective agreements or agreements concluded between the two sides of industry at a lower level.

Member States in which there is no statutory system ensuring the conclusion of collective agreements or agreements concluded between the two sides of industry at national or regional level, on the matters covered by this Directive, or those Member States in which there is a specific legislative framework for this purpose and within the limits thereof, may, in accordance with national legislation and/or practice, allow derogations from Articles 3, 4, 5, 8 and 16 by way of collective agreements or agreements concluded between the two sides of industry at the appropriate collective level.

The derogations provided for in the first and second subparagraphs shall be allowed on condition that equivalent compensating rest periods are granted to the workers concerned or, in exceptional cases where it is not possible for objective reasons to grant such periods, the workers concerned are afforded appropriate protection.

Member States may lay down rules:

— for the application of this paragraph by the two sides of industry, and

— for the extension of the provisions of collective agreements or agreements concluded in conformity with this paragraph to other workers in accordance with national legislation and/or practice.

4.   The option to derogate from point 2 of Article 16, provided in paragraph 2, points 2.1. and 2.2. and in paragraph 3 of this Article, may not result in the establishment of a reference period exceeding six months.

However, Member States shall have the option, subject to compliance with the general principles relating to the protection of the safety and health of workers, of allowing, for objective or technical reasons or reasons concerning the organization of work, collective agreements or agreements concluded between the two sides of industry to set reference periods in no event exceeding 12 months.

Before the expiry of a period of seven years from the date referred to in Article 18(1)(a), the Council shall, on the basis of a Commission proposal accompanied by an appraisal report, re-examine the provisions of this paragraph and decide what action to take.

Article 18

Final provisions

1.   (a) Member States shall adopt the laws, regulations and administrative provisions necessary to comply with this Directive by 23 November 1996, or shall

ensure by that date that the two sides of industry establish the necessary measures by agreement, with Member States being obliged to take any necessary steps to enable them to guarantee at all times that the provisions laid down by this Directive are fulfilled.

(b)(i) However, a Member State shall have the option not to apply Article 6, while respecting the general principles of the protection of the safety and health of workers, and provided it takes the necessary measures to ensure that:

— no employer requires a worker to work more than 48 hours over a seven-day period, calculated as an average for the reference period referred to in point 2 of Article 16, unless he has first obtained the worker's agreement to perform such work,

— no worker is subjected to any detriment by his employer because he is not willing to give his agreement to perform such work,

— the employer keeps up-to-date records of all workers who carry out such work,

— the records are placed at the disposal of the competent authorities, which may, for reasons connected with the safety and/or health of workers, prohibit or restrict the possibility of exceeding the maximum weekly working hours,

— the employer provides the competent authorities at their request with information on cases in which agreement has been given by workers to perform work exceeding 48 hours over a period of seven days, calculated as an average for the reference period referred to in point 2 of Article 16.

Before the expiry of a period of seven years from the date referred to in (a), the Council shall, on the basis of a Commission proposal accompanied by an appraisal report, re-examine the provisions of this point (i) and decide on what action to take.

(ii) Similarly, Member States shall have the option, as regards the application of Article 7, of making use of a transitional period of not more than three years from the date referred to in (a), provided that during that transitional period:

— every worker receives three weeks' paid annual leave in accordance with the conditions for the entitlement to, and granting of, such leave laid down by national legislation and/or practice, and

— the three-week period of paid annual leave may not be replaced by an allowance in lieu, except where the employment relationship is terminated.

(c) Member states shall forthwith inform the Commission thereof.

2. When Member States adopt the measures referred to in paragraph 1, they shall contain a reference to this Directive or shall be accompanied by such reference on the occasion of their official publication. The methods of making such a reference shall be laid down by the Member States.

3. Without prejudice to the right of Member States to develop, in the light of changing circumstances, different legislative, regulatory or contractual provisions in the field of working time, as long as the minimum requirements provided for in this Directive are complied with, implementation of this Directive shall not constitute valid grounds for reducing the general level of protection afforded to workers.

4. Member States shall communicate to the Commission the texts of the provisions of national law already adopted or being adopted in the field governed by this Directive.

5. Member States shall report to the Commission every five years on the practical implementation of the provisions of this Directive, indicating the viewpoints of the two sides of industry.

The Commission shall inform the European Parliament, the Council, the Economic and Social Committee and the Advisory Committee on Safety, Hygiene and Health Protection at Work thereof.

6. Every five years the Commission shall submit to the European Parliament, the Council and the Economic and Social Committee a report on the application of this Directive taking into account paragraphs 1, 2, 3, 4 and 5.

Article 19

This Directive is addressed to the Member States.

Done at Brussels, 23 November 1993.

For the Council
The President
M. SMET

Appendix Three
Text of the Young Workers Directive

COUNCIL DIRECTIVE 94/33/EC
of 22 June 1994
on the protection of young people at work

THE COUNCIL OF THE EUROPEAN UNION,

Having regard to the Treaty establishing the European Community, and in particular Article 118a thereof,

Having regard to the proposal from the Commission,

Having regard to the opinion of the Economic and Social Committee,

Acting in accordance with the procedure referred to in Article 189c of the Treaty,

Whereas Article 118a of the Treaty provides that the Council shall adopt, by means of Directives, minimum requirements to encourage improvements, especially in the working environment, as regards the health and safety of workers;

Whereas, under that Article, such Directives must avoid imposing administrative, financial and legal constraints in a way which would hold back the creation and development of small and medium-sized undertakings;

Whereas points 20 and 22 of the Community Charter of the Fundamental Social Rights of Workers, adopted by the European Council in Strasbourg on 9 December 1989, state that:

'20. Without prejudice to such rules as may be more favourable to young people, in particular those ensuring their preparation for work through vocational training, and subject to derogations limited to certain light work, the minimum employment age must not be lower than the minimum school-leaving age and, in any case, not lower than 15 years;

22. Appropriate measures must be taken to adjust labour regulations applicable to young workers so that their specific development and vocational training and access to employment needs are met.

The duration of work must, in particular, be limited — without it being possible to circumvent this limitation through recourse to overtime — and night work prohibited in the case of workers of under eighteen years of age, save in the case of certain jobs laid down in national legislation or regulations.';

Whereas account should be taken of the principles of the International Labour Organization regarding the protection of young people at work, including those relating to the minimum age for access to employment or work;

Whereas, in this Resolution on child labour, the European Parliament summarized the various aspects of work by young people and stressed its effects on their health, safety and physical and intellectual development, and pointed to the need to adopt a Directive harmonizing national legislation in the field;

Whereas Article 15 of Council Directive 89/391/EEC of 12 June 1989 on the introduction of measures to encourage improvements in the safety and health of workers at work provides that particularly sensitive risk groups must be protected against the dangers which specifically affect them;

Whereas children and adolescents must be considered specific risk groups, and measures must be taken with regard to their safety and health;

Whereas the vulnerability of children calls for Member States to prohibit their employment and ensure that the minimum working or employment age is not lower than the minimum age at which compulsory schooling as imposed by national law ends or 15 years in any event; whereas derogations from the prohibition on child labour may be admitted only in special cases and under the conditions stipulated in this Directive; whereas, under no circumstances, may such derogations be detrimental to regular school attendance or prevent children benefiting fully from their education;

Whereas, in view of the nature of the transition from childhood to adult life, work by adolescents should be strictly regulated and protected;

Whereas every employer should guarantee young people working conditions appropriate to their age;

Whereas employers should implement the measures necessary to protect the safety and health of young people on the basis on an assessment of work-related hazards to the young;

Whereas Member States should protect young people against any specific risks arising from their lack of experience, absence of awareness of existing or potential risks, or from their immaturity;

Whereas Member States should therefore prohibit the employment of young people for the work specified by this Directive;

Whereas the adoption of specific minimal requirements in respect of the organization of working time is likely to improve working conditions for young people;

Whereas the maximum working time of young people should be strictly limited and night work by young people should be prohibited, with the exception of certain jobs specified by national legislation or rules;

Whereas Member States should take the appropriate measures to ensure that the working time of adolescents receiving school education does not adversely affect their ability to benefit from that education;

Whereas time spent on training by young persons working under a theoretical and/or practical combined work/training scheme or an in-plant work-experience should be counted as working time;

Whereas, in order to ensure the safety and health of young people, the latter should be granted minimum daily, weekly and annual periods of rest and adequate breaks;

Whereas, with respect to the weekly rest period, due account should be taken of the diversity of cultural, ethnic, religious and other factors prevailing in the Member States; whereas in particular, it is ultimately for each Member State to decide whether Sunday should be included in the weekly rest period, and if so to what extent;

Whereas appropriate work experience may contribute to the aim of preparing young people for adult working and social life, provided it is ensured that any harm to their safety, health and development is avoided;

Whereas, although derogations from the bans and limitations imposed by this Directive would appear indispensable for certain activities or particular situations, applications thereof must not prejudice the principles underlying the established protection system;

Whereas this Directive constitutes a tangible step towards developing the social dimension of the internal market;

Whereas the application in practice of the system of protection laid down by this Directive will require that Member States implement a system of effective and proportionate measures;

Whereas the implementation of some provisions of this Directive poses particular problems for one Member State with regard to its system of protection for young people at work; whereas that Member State should therefore be allowed to refrain from implementing the relevant provisions for a suitable period,

HAS ADOPTED THIS DIRECTIVE:

SECTION I

Article 1

Purpose

1. Member States shall take the necessary measures to prohibit work by children.

They shall ensure, under the conditions laid down by this Directive, that the minimum working or employment age is not lower than the minimum age at which compulsory full-time schooling as imposed by national law ends or 15 years in any event.

2. Member States ensure that work by adolescents is strictly regulated and protected under the conditions laid down in this Directive.

3. Member States shall ensure in general that employers guarantee that young people have working conditions which suit their age.

They shall ensure that young people are protected against economic exploitation and against any work likely to harm their safety, health or physical, mental, moral or social development or to jeopardize their education.

Article 2

Scope

1. This Directive shall apply to any person under 18 years of age having an employment contract or an employment relationship defined by the law in force in a Member State and/or governed by the law in force in a Member State.

2. Member States may make legislative or regulatory provision for this Directive not to apply, within the limits and under the conditions which they set by legislative or regulatory provision, to occasional work or short-term work involving:

(a)   domestic service in a private household, or
(b)   work regarded as not being harmful, damaging or dangerous to young people in a family undertaking.

Article 3

Definitons

For the purposes of this Directive:
(a)   'young person' shall mean any person under 18 years of age referred to in Article 2 (1);
(b)   'child' shall mean any young person of less than 15 years of age or who is still subject to compulsory full-time schooling under national law;
(c)   'adolescent' shall mean any young person of at least 15 years of age but less than 18 years of age who is no longer subject to compulsory full-time schooling under national law; .
(d)   'light work' shall mean all work which, on account of the inherent nature of the tasks which it involves and the particular conditions under which they are performed:
(i)   is not likely to be harmful to the safety, health or development of children, and
(ii)   is not such as to be harmful to their attendance at school, their participation in vocational guidance or training programmes approved by the competent authority or their capacity to benefit from the instruction received;
(e)   'working time' shall mean any period during which the young person is at work, at the employer's disposal and carrying out his activity or duties in accordance with national legislation and/or practice;
(f)   'rest period' shall mean any period which is not working time.

Article 4

Prohibition of work by children

1.   Member States shall adopt the measures necessary to prohibit work by children.
2.   Taking into account the objectives set out in Article 1, Member States may make legislative or regulatory provision for the prohibition of work by children not to apply to:
(a)   children pursuing the activities set out in Article 5;
(b)   children of at least 14 years of age working under a combined work/training scheme or an in-plant work-experience scheme, provided that such work is done in accordance with the conditions laid down by the competent authority;
(c)   children of at least 14 years of age performing light work other than that covered by Article 5; light work other than that covered by Article 5 may, however, be performed by children of 13 years of age for a limited number of hours per week in the case of categories of work determined by national legislation.
3.   Member States that make use of the option referred to in paragraph 2(c) shall determine, subject to the provisions of this Directive, the working conditions relating to the light work in question.

Article 5

Cultural or similar activities

1. The employment of children for the purposes of performance in cultural, artistic, sports or advertising activities shall be subject to prior authorization to be given by the competent authority in individual çases.

2. Member States shall by legislative or regulatory provision lay down the working conditions for children in the cases referred to in paragraph 1 and the details of the prior authorization procedure, on condition that the activities:

(i) are not likely to be harmful to the safety, health or development of children, and

(ii) are not such as to be harmful to their attendance at school, their participation in vocational guidance or training programmes approved by the competent authority or their capacity to benefit from the instruction received.

3. By way of derogation from the procedure laid down in paragraph 1, in the case of children of at least 13 years of age, Member States may authorize, by legislative or regulatory provision, in accordance with conditions which they shall determine, the employment of children for the purposes of performance in cultural, artistic, sports or advertising activities.

4. The Member States which have a specific authorization system for modelling agencies with regard to the activities of children may retain that system.

SECTION II

Article 6

General obligations on employers

1. Without prejudice to Article 4(1), the employer shall adopt the measures necessary to protect the safety and health of young people, taking particular account of the specific risks referred to in Article 7(1).

2. The employer shall implement the measures provided for in paragraph 1 on the basis of an assessment of the hazards to young people in connection with their work.

The assessment must be made before young people begin work and when there is any major change in working conditions and must pay particular attention to the following points:

(a) the fitting-out and layout of the workplace and the workstation;

(b) the nature, degree and duration of exposure to physical, biological and chemical agents;

(c) the form, range and use of work equipment, in particular agents, machines, apparatus and devices, and the way in which they are handled;

(d) the arrangement of work processes and operations and the way in which these are combined (organization of work);

(e) the level of training and instruction given to young people.

Where this assessment shows that there is a risk to the safety, the physical or mental health or development of young people, an appropriate free assessment and monitoring of their health shall be provided at regular intervals without prejudice to Directive 89/391/EEC.

The free health assessment and monitoring may form part of a national health system.

3. The employer shall inform young people of possible risks and of all measures adopted concerning their safety and health.

Furthermore, he shall inform the legal representatives of children of possible risks and of all measures adopted concerning children's safety and health.

4. The employer shall involve the protective and preventive services referred to in Article 7 of Directive 89/391/EEC in the planning, implementation and monitoring of the safety and health conditions applicable to young people.

Article 7

Vulnerability of young people — Prohibition of work

1. Member States shall ensure that young people are protected from any specific risks to their safety, health and development which are a consequence of their lack of experience, of absence of awareness of existing or potential risks or of the fact that young people have not yet fully matured.

2. Without prejudice to Article 4(1), Member States shall to this end prohibit the employment of young people for:

(a) work which is objectively beyond their physical or psychological capacity;

(b) work involving harmful exposure to agents which are toxic, carcinogenic, cause heritable genetic damage, or harm to the unborn child or which in any other way chronically affect human health;

(c) work involving harmful exposure to radiation;

(d) work involving the risk of accidents which it may be assumed cannot be recognized or avoided by young persons owing to their insufficient attention to safety or lack of experience or training; or

(e) work in which there is a risk to health from extreme cold or heat, or from noise or vibration.

Work which is likely to entail specific risks for young people within the meaning of paragraph 1 includes:

— work involving harmful exposure to the physical, biological and chemical agents referred to in point I of the Annex, and

— processes and work referred to in point II of the Annex.

3. Member States may, by legislative or regulatory provision, authorize derogations from paragraph 2 in the case of adolescents where such derogations are indispensable for their vocational training, provided that protection of their safety and health is ensured by the fact that the work is performed under the supervision of a competent person within the meaning of Article 7 of Directive 89/391/EEC and provided that the protection afforded by that Directive is guaranteed.

SECTION III

Article 8

Working time

1. Member States which make use of the option in Article 4(2)(b) or (c) shall adopt the measures necessary to limit the working time of children to:

(a) eight hours a day and 40 hours a week for work performed under a combined work/training scheme or an in-plant work-experience scheme;

(b) two hours on a school day and 12 hours a week for work performed in term-time outside the hours fixed for school attendance, provided that this is not prohibited by national legislation and/or practice; in no circumstances may the daily working time exceed seven hours; this limit may be raised to eight hours in the case of children who have reached the age of 15;

(c) seven hours a day and 35 hours a week for work performed during a period of at least a week when school is not operating; these limits may be raised to eight hours a day and 40 hours a week in the case of chidren who have reached the age of 15;

(d) seven hours a day and 35 hours a week for light work performed by children no longer subject to compulsory full-time schooling under national law.

2. Member States shall adopt the measures necessary to limit the working time of adolescents to eight hours a day and 40 hours a week.

3. The time spent on training by a young person working under a theoretical and/or practical combined work/training scheme or an in-plant work-experience scheme shall be counted as working time.

4. Where a young person is employed by more than one employer, working days and working time shall be cumulative.

5. Member States may, by legislative or regulatory provision, authorize derogations from paragraph 1(a) and paragraph 2 either by way of exception or where there are objective grounds for so doing.

Member States shall, by legislative or regulatory provision, determine the conditions, limits and procedure for implementing such derogations.

Article 9

Night work

1. (a) Member States which make use of the option in Article 4(2)(b) or (c) shall adopt the measures necessary to prohibit work by children between 8 p.m. and 6 a.m.

(b) Member States shall adopt the measures necessary to prohibit work by adolescents either between 10 p.m. and 6 a.m. or between 11 p.m. and 7 a.m.

2. (a) Member States may, by legislative or regulatory provision, authorize work by adolescents in specific areas of activity during the period in which night work is prohibited as referred to in paragraph 1(b).

In that event, Member States shall take appropriate measures to ensure that the adolescent is supervised by an adult where such supervision is necessary for the adolescent's protection.

(b) If point (a) is applied, work shall continue to be prohibited between midnight and 4 a.m.

However, Member States may, by legislative or regulatory provision, authorize work by adolescents during the period in which night work is prohibited in the following cases, where there are objective grounds for so doing and provided that adolescents are allowed suitable compensatory rest time and that the objectives set out in Article 1 are not called into question:

— work performed in the shipping or fisheries sectors;
— work performed in the context of the armed forces or the police;
— work performed in hospitals or similar establishments;
— cultural, artistic, sports or advertising activities.

3. Prior to any assignment to night work and at regular intervals thereafter, adolescents shall be entitled to a free assessment of their health and capacities, unless the work they do during the period during which work is prohibited is of an exceptional nature.

Article 10

Rest period

1. (a)   Member States which make use of the option in Article 4(2)(b) or (c) shall adopt the measures necessary to ensure that, for each 24-hour period, children are entitled to a minimum rest period of 14 consecutive hours.

(b)   Member States shall adopt the measures necessary to ensure that, for each 24-hour period, adolescents are entitled to a minimum rest period of 12 consecutive hours.

2. Member States shall adopt the measures necessary to ensure that, for each seven-day period:
— children in respect of whom they have made use of the option in Article 4(2)(b) or (c), and
— adolescents
are entitled to a minimum rest period of two days, which shall be consecutive if possible.

Where justified by technical or organization reasons, the minimum rest period may be reduced, but may in no circumstances be less than 36 consecutive hours.

The minimum rest period referred to in the first and second subparagraphs shall in principle include Sunday.

3. Member States may, by legislative or regulatory provision, provide for the minimum rest periods referred to in pargraphs 1 and 2 to be interrupted in the case of activities involving periods of work that are split up over the day or are of short duration.

4. Member States may make legislative or regulatory provision for derogations from paragraph 1(b) and paragraph 2 in respect of adolescents in the following cases, where there are objective grounds for so doing and provided that they are granted appropriate compensatory rest time and that the objectives set out in Article 1 are not called into question:

(a)   work performed in the shipping or fisheries sectors;

(b)   work performed in the context of the armed forces or the police;

(c)   work performed in hospitals or similar establishments;

(d)   work performed in agriculture;

(e)   work performed in the tourism industry or in the hotel, restaurant and café sector;

(f)   activities involving periods of work split up over the day.

Article 11

Annual rest

Member States which make use of the option referred to in Article 4(2)(b) or (c) shall see to it that a period free of any work is included, as far as possible, in the school holidays of children subject to compulsory full-time schooling under national law.

Article 12

Breaks

Member States shall adopt the measures necessary to ensure that, where daily working time is more than four and a half hours, young people are entitled to a break of at least 30 minutes, which shall be consecutive if possible.

Article 13

Work by adolescents in the event of *force majeure*

Member States may, by legislative or regulatory provision, authorize derogations from Article 8(2), Article 9(1)(b), Article 10(1)(b) and, in the case of adolescents, Article 12, for work in the circumstances referred to in Article 5(4) of Directive 89/391/EEC, provided that such work is of a temporary nature and must be performed immediately, that adult workers are not available and that the adolescents are allowed equivalent compensatory rest time within the following three weeks.

SECTION IV

Article 14

Measures

Each Member State shall lay down any necessary measures to be applied in the event of failure to comply with the provisions adopted in order to implement this . Directive; such measures must be effective and proportionate.

Article 15

Adaptation of the Annex

Adaptations of a strictly technical nature to the Annex in the light of technical progress, changes in international rules or specifications and advances in knowledge in the field covered by this Directive shall be adopted in accordance with the procedure provided for in Article 17 of Directive 89/391/EEC.

Article 16

Non-reducing clause

Without prejudice to the right of Member States to develop, in the light of changing circumstances, different provisions on the protection of young people, as long as the minimum requirements provided for by this Directive are complied with, the implementation of this Directive shall not constitute valid grounds for reducing the general level of protection afforded to young people.

Article 17

Final provisions

1.   (a)   Member States shall bring into force the laws, regulations and administrative provisions necessary to comply with this Directive not later than 22 June 1996 or ensure, by that date at the latest, that the two sides of industry introduce the requisite provisions by means of collective agreements, with Member States

being required to make all the necessary provisions to enable them at all times to guarantee the results laid down by this Directive.

(b)   The United Kingdom may refrain from implementing the first subparagraph of Article 8(1)(b) with regard to the provision relating to the maximum weekly working time, and also Article 8(2) and Article 9(1)(b) and (2) for a period of four years from the date specified in subparagraph (a).

The Commission shall submit a report on the effects of this provision.

The Council, acting in accordance with the conditions laid down by the Treaty, shall decide whether this period should be extended.

(c)   Member States shall forthwith inform the Commission thereof.

2.   When Member States adopt the measures referred to in paragraph 1, such measures shall contain a reference to this Directive or shall be accompanied by such reference on the occasion of their official publication. The methods of making such reference shall be laid down by Member States.

3.   Member States shall communicate to the Commission the texts of the main provisions of national law which they have already adopted or adopt in the field governed by this Directive.

4.   Member States shall report to the Commission every five years on the practical implementation of the provisions of this Directive, indicating the viewpoints of the two sides of industry.

The Commission shall inform the European Parliament, the Council and the Economic and Social Committee thereof.

5.   The Commission shall periodically submit to the European Parliament, the Council and the Economic and Social Committee a report on the application of this Directive taking into account pargraphs 1, 2, 3 and 4.

Article 18

This Directive is addressed to the Member States.

Done at Luxembourg, 22 June 1994.

For the Council
The President
E. YIANNOPOULOS

Annex

Non-exhaustive list of agents, processes and work (Article 7(2), second subparagraph)

I. Agents
1. Physical agents
   (a) Ionizing radiation;
   (b) Work in a high-pressure atmosphere, e.g. in pressurized containers, diving.
2. Biological agents
   (a) Biological agents belonging to groups 3 and 4 within the meaning of Article 2(d) of Council Directive 90/679/EEC of 26 November 1990 on the protection of workers from risks related to exposure to biological agents at work (Seventh individual Directive within the meaning of Article 16(1) of Directive 89/391/EEC).
3. Chemical agents
   (a) Substances and preparations classified according to Council Directive 67/548/EEC of 27 June 1967 on the approximation of laws, regulations and administrative provisions relating to the classification, packaging and labelling of dangerous substances with amendments and Council Directive 88/379/EEC of 7 June 1988 on the approximation of the laws, regulations and administrative provisions of the Member States relating to the classification, packaging and labelling of dangerous preparations as toxic (T), very toxic (Tx), corrosive (C) or explosive (E);
   (b) Substances and preparations classified according to Directives 67/548/EEC and 88/379/EEC as harmful (Xn) and with one or more of the following risk phrases:
— danger of very serious irreversible effects (R39),
— possible risk of irreversible effects (R40),
— may cause sensitization by inhalation (R42),
— may cause sensitization by skin contact (R43),
— may cause cancer (R45),
— may cause heritable genetic damage (R46),
— danger of serious damage to health by prolonged exposure (R48),
— may impair fertility (R60),
— may cause harm to the unborn child (R61);
   (c) Substances and preparations classified according to Directives 67/548/EEC and 88/379/EEC as irritant (Xi) and with one or more of the following risk phrases:
— highly flammable (R12);
— may cause sensitization by inhalation (R42),
— may cause sensitization by skin contact (R43),
   (d) Substances and preparations referred to Article 2 (c) of Council Directive 90/394/EEC of 28 June 1990 on the protection of workers from the risks related to exposure to carcinogens at work (Sixth individual Directive within the meaning of Article 16(1) of Directive 89/391/EEC;
   (e) Lead and compounds thereof, inasmuch as the agents in question are absorbable by the human organism;
   (f) Asbestos.

II.   Processes and work

1.   Processes at work referred to in Annex I to Directive 90/394/EEC.

2.   Manufacture and handling of devices, fireworks or other objects containing explosives.

3.   Work with fierce or poisonous animals.

4.   Animal slaughtering on an industrial scale.

5.   Work involving the handling of equipment for the production, storage or application of compressed, liquified or dissolved gases.

6.   Work with vats, tanks, reservoirs or carboys containing chemical agents referred to in 1.3.

7.   Work involving a risk of structural collapse.

8.   Work involving high-voltage electrical hazards.

9.   Work the pace of which is determined by machinery and involving payment by results.

Index